TURN TO THE EAST

TURN TO THE EAST

by two who seek here to intimate
the richness of their
adventure

CAROLINE SINGER
and
C. LE ROY BALDRIDGE

MINTON, BALCH & COMPANY
NEW YORK
1926

PRINTED IN THE UNITED STATES
BY THE PRINTING HOUSE OF WILLIAM EDWIN RUDGE
MOUNT VERNON · NEW YORK

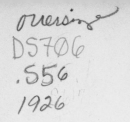
Foreword

IT IS not unfitting that I introduce this volume. Perhaps I am not over-assuming in claiming for myself a certain kinship to it. For it was in response to my importunities that Roy Baldridge first came out to China from the war in 1919. My proselyting was not inspired by personal desires alone. China offers inexhaustible delights to an artist. To him it offers also the richness of long accumulated aesthetic tradition. So Roy Baldridge first saw the vulgar but colorful intermingling of civilizations in Shanghai, the timeless poise of the Shantung mountains and the majestic glories of Peking with me as cicerone.

Once having lived in China the traveller back home inevitably finds himself filled with a homesickness, a longing to return. The second trip of Roy Baldridge was with his wife, Caroline Singer. Their year in Japan, Korea and China has resulted in this book. Not one book, I should say, but two. It is neither a volume of travel essays illustrated by the author's husband nor a volume of sketches with text by the artist's wife. No two pairs of eyes can see alike in the East, no two imaginations respond alike to what the eyes report. So here are rendered in two different media, brought together because they are complementary, the imprint of the East on two different personalities.

It is no easy task, this rendering. Only the dull rush heedlessly into print with "impressions of the Orient." To those with more sensitive perceptions the East is too overwhelming for easy articulateness. It intimidates. The first few hours in Peking not only confuse, they frighten. Color is too vivid, motion in too unfamiliar a rhythm, mass too imposing, the content of the life about one too alien for translation into terms intelligible to the Western mind. Another barrier also intervenes: the prejudices of the foreign residents. To escape the influence of either their over-enthusiasm or maladjustment is difficult for one thrown suddenly into an alien culture.

This task of setting down, without prejudice, what they each perceived, confining themselves entirely to their own intimate experiences, is not easy. And yet—as cicerone to Roy Baldridge, by proxy to Caroline Singer, I make my claim of kinship to this book not without pride.

NATHANIEL PEFFER.

New York City, 1926.

The Capricious Nightingale

AS UNSEEN hands draw back the Japanese theater's striped curtain upon the first act of love's tragedy a hidden flute proclaims that love is doomed. At nightfall ragged minstrels pipe, calling pretty ladies who sing and dance for hire to railings of the tea-house balconies, telling them that life is brief and filled with woe. Far-off sobbing of a flute awakens the sleeper. At dawn, priests, richly robed mendicants, their heads completely concealed by wicker masks, quaver and cry upon their flutes for alms. Piercing and attenuated, formless as a revery, this unspun music floats across my senses as in a garden misty unspun filaments of cobweb drift across eyelids and cheeks, brushing them with eerie finger-tips. In this there is for me enchantment. And so tonight I follow the Japanese author up and up a narrow street which is filled with the pungence of dust upon which clean cold water is thrown from doorways by little people in kimonos. There walks here tonight a master of the flute, come to aid a gentleman in the recovery of his soul.

Humble this street is, but not mean, for it is a pathway to the maple forests of Kiyomizu, and down its narrow steepness, past the paper windows, roll quivering golden hoops of sound, the music of the temple's gongs. Into a house like a child's playhouse I go, stooping, for the door is low. A toy staircase leads from a pair of rooms below to a pair above. From the padded matting upon the floor there exudes a dry odor like singed grass. There is no furniture. For seats there are floor cushions covered with figured cotton. A gourd-shaped clay pot and a scroll in a niche are the only ornaments. Between the pairs of rooms a courtyard no larger than a cupboard is open to the sky. Forest and mountain pool are intimated by plumes of young bamboo, a dwarfed pine, squat and contorted, beside a hollowed rock in which goldfish glitter. In an open door-way upon the courtyard's ledge sits the flute-player.

He is beautiful. He is not like the common man with short thick body, straight

3

The narrow way to Kiyomizu

slits of eyes set above square cheeks, flattened nose, and protruding upper lip which draws back in speech or laughter baring teeth and gums. The eyes, set in an oval face of soft contours, slant beneath whimsical brows. High and thin, his nose is also slightly hooked. Such a face I have seen carved upon a Nō mask of unknown origin. The shining black hair brushed away from his face lies long upon his neck. Set high and close to his head the ears are slightly pointed. Beautiful he is as are the dancers and actors of Tokyo who pass from masculine to feminine rôles, being when they choose more exquisitely womanish than any woman. But he is not pale as they are pale, exotic indoor men. Deep into his flesh have sunk the colors of sunlight and sea-air, of moonlight and mountain-peaks.

He does not sit as the others do, kneeling upon floor-cushions, feet flattened beneath them, but contrives to sit high upon his heels. This posture affirms his aloofness. A look of dignity is enhanced by a divided skirt of dark grey stuff drawn over his grey kimono and arranged about him stiffly in the manner of a noble's costume upon the stage. Motionless he sits and will not look at me but looks beyond my head as captive wild things sometimes look beyond those who stare at them. Captive he is not, but to some extent he has been tricked. Doubtless I merit this disdain. Warned that he is subject to quick and inexplicable moods, that he is hostile to foreigners, I have come here without his invitation hoping to hear him play upon the flute. In no other way can I hear him. I am told that recently he refused further to record his music, saying that the flute is for those who will play it, not for Japanese who are content with music thrown off whirling discs.

This rendez-vous was arranged between the author, my friend, and the grey-haired gentleman, our host, who is the flute-player's pupil. In official circles of the capital this old gentleman enjoyed, not long ago, a position of security. Suddenly he became possessed of an awareness, I am told. The capital's life appeared to him a highly colored and meaningless merry-go-round, speeding in circles to a hideous tune, himself a dizzy rider in foreign frock coat and high hat, arriving nowhere. His life was neither wholly foreign nor wholly Japanese.

4

Kiyomizu

He fled. Accompanied by his wife, who sits beside him with that look of eternal acquiescence, he lives frugally, dresses as poorly as a laborer and devotes himself to contemplative Buddhism and to the flute. This instrument he chose of all the others because it is most truly Oriental. He is old but when he dies a Japanese will die and not a fretted creature uncertain of his identity.

To dissipate the master musician's aloofness I am told by the author to ask some courteous question which he will convey. This is embarrassing. Any question will reveal my interest as arising out of the shallows of curiosity and not out of the depths of information. In a cloth bag beside him the flute lies. If he is to play, the flute must be tactfully got out of that bag. May I see it? As if hinged only at the hips, he bows. The flute, two pieces of polished bamboo, barren of metal and joined together, is examined, admired. From bamboo which he cut himself he carved this flute and so must every flute-player carve his own, changing the instrument until it responds to his innermost personality. So intimate an expression is flute-playing that by the first note the master believes he can determine the character of any player. He passes the flute to me. I am to be judged. I grow hot with exertion, cold with humiliation. But there comes no sound other than the futile whistling of my own breath. Obviously for him I cannot exist. And as I return the instrument I suspect a fine-edged malice sparkling in his eyes and along the lines of his lips.

Will he now play so that I in turn may judge? He lifts the flute and one weeping note creeps through the house. In the distance a motor horn brays, a trolley car rattles, wooden clogs follow wooden clogs in an incessant murmur up the hill. Quivering golden hoops of sound roll by the paper windows. With a whisper the surface of the pool breaks as the goldfish leap. Will he play? Like the nerves of a person who crouches hour after hour beneath a hedge awaiting the capricious nightingale, my nerves are taut with expectation. Will he play? My nerves relax; for he has lifted up the flute. Deliberately he toots eight notes of a familiar scale—his little joke. Then he gives to us a chain of tones delicately linked, one into another, the thirty-six tones, he says, of the ancient scale, a scale

5

which few can play and almost none can hear since Japanese prefer foreign fiddles and music-machines. Long before the scale was thus simplified a Korean prince who carved his own flute like any other man drew from it three thousand tones! Will he play? I think so. The author conveys to him my extravagant appreciation of the scales, my enthusiasms for the Korean prince. From his hips the flute-player bows. He pulls apart his flute. Into the bag the two pieces are thrust and the puckering string jerked with unmistakable finality.

Unaccustomed to kneeling, I scramble awkwardly to my feet. At the same time I must remember to stoop or crash my head into the ceiling. My confusion is great. While I fumble over my slippers in the entry I hear that the flute-player is saying something to my companion. Down the hill we walk towards the metropolitan blaze of electricity in which the humble street is lost. I am given a message. To the foreign woman the master flute-player says that when she has heard the bamboo flute played in a bamboo forest with no other sound except the song of the leaves, with no other light than the moon, then only will she understand the invisible undercurrent of the Orient, then will she understand the soul of a Japanese.

A Japanese Gentleman's Night Out

THE sun is down. Along the hill-tops from an incredible distance, trees like burnt matches are visible against a tremulous band of topaz and pale green, a lingering band of light dividing dark earth from a darkening sky upon which already a few sharp-edged stars are carved. Behind paper windows quiver the strings of native guitars. Like night birds, drummers cry out, while hidden women with bare, dancing feet make audible the passionate pulse of a Kyoto night.

At this hour the street of geisha-houses is filled with perfumed agitation,

6

R. B. Kyoto '24

Where the well-to-do
Japanese gentlemen
spend their nights out.

Bright colored
toys for
Japanese
Gentlemen

C.LeRoy Baldridge
-Kyoto- '25

heavy scents from flower-colored garments, incense, and twinkling hair-orna-ments. Fresh from the hands of their dressers, the eyes of their masters and mistresses, the childish bondwomen, handmaidens of the night, bright-colored toys for gentlemen, saunter, or are carried off, two by two, in double rickshaws. At the same hour docile, kneeling wives who have passed, garment by garment, to their husbands, clothes for evening wear, now watch them depart for the tea-houses upon the river bank.

Married women do not accompany their husbands to tea-houses, although a gentleman may stay the night if he wishes, if he can afford it. Foreigners are unwelcome; for the balconies beneath which the water whispers and gurgles are the exclusive playground of Japanese men. That we remain for several days in this one is due to Madame's weakness for the arts. One of us paints. Also she has a certain special tenderness for her old friends, the painter and the potter, by whom we were brought. Moreover, it need not be known that she has harbored foreigners this little while, the house being, it is said, tactfully winked at by the police, since not infrequently a prince, incognito, sits upon Madame's balconies and calls upon her to produce the costliest and most beautiful dancing girl.

The permanent residents are an old crone in the kitchen and the maids. Re-ceiving no wages these depend upon tips given them in the colored envelopes which guests carry for this purpose. Having no room they may not rest until the last guest is either gone away or abed. Then wherever there is floor-space, in the hall, in a vacant room, in the bedding closet, they unroll their mats. A school-girl, the pale child of Madame, kneels in the shadows watching with weary eyes. A cough too pitifully explains her gentle lassitude. Like the maids, having no room, she, too, may not rest until the front door is at last barred and in the air-tight entry she sinks down upon a mattress beside her mother.

The eyes of Madame are relentless like the eyes of one who has for many years pressed a dark wine of life from the petty follies of men and the helpless-ness of her own sex. Heavy with living are face and body, and yet there is also something self-possessed and almost queenly as she passes from balcony to

8

KYOTO
- 24 -

Restaurant
Women

R. B.
at Shibata's
TOKYO/25

Forest Shrines

C Le Roy Baldridge
— NIKKO '25 —

balcony, placing the lanterns, gauze buds enfolding candles, rising upon black lacquer stems within the dim circles of light which they cast upon the floor.

I am somewhat troublesome to this woman. To her world there could be nothing more alien, more monstrous than a wife accompanying her husband, a woman neither docile nor kneeling, a woman six feet tall and with hair cut short. Once and for all she sets me outside that world, her pretty manners thinly veneering her antagonism. At her bidding, the maid each evening after the bath enwraps my nakedness. The black and white kimono belted by a dark ribbon is the costume furnished by tea-houses to men guests! But thus am I clothed in magic; for so long as I remain quiet in the darkest corners, I am unnoticed. Madame has clothed me in invisibility.

The sound of hand-clapping in a tea-house indicates that some gentleman's desires have become articulate. Madame, accompanied by a maid, presents herself. What does the honorable sir wish? Madame and the maid bow and bow again. Cigarettes, a bath, fruit packed in sugar and shaved ice, dinner, dancing girls, courtesans? There is no reservation. And already this evening Madame has procured three handsome courtesans, women whose freedom has bred a pleasing vivacity, for three handsome lads. These boys, wealthy students, are of the new type, long-limbed, muscular, tall as Europeans and wide-eyed; accustomed to foreign chairs, foreign beds, imported foods, athletics and hats shading their eyes. Having dined they now wriggle out of their kimonos and sit half-naked in the soft night air. Upon their gleaming backs the three courtesans beat their hands in unison. To the rhythm of flat, smacking blows they recite couplets, evidently risqué; for, sitting here beside me, Madame, the painter and the potter listening intently, laugh covertly but with relish. If this be rowdiness, it is evidently of an orderly and permissible variety, as smacking blows and chanting can be heard in tea-houses all up and down the river bank. Otherwise the men and women exchange no caresses. They do not touch one another. They do not so much as touch one another's garments.

Using Madame's ink and brushes, the painter and potter with cunning strokes

10

Acrobat and Singers

R. B.—Theatre Street
KYOTO '24

C·LeRoy Baldridge – PEKING/25

In stiff bright silks
the generation flowers
against a background
of decayed splendor.

intimate, rather than draw, upon the blank fans which she has brought, a bearded philosopher alone in a boat upon a lonely sea, two absurd and fuzzy ducklings, the inevitable birds, flowers, bamboo, and butterflies. These are souvenirs for Madame. But her rapturous admiration of the arts is abruptly checked by business. The breathless maid announces an arrival.

At the end of the corridor is a pompous person in tailored tweeds whom the maid ushers into the bath. After scrubbing his back and drying his person as if he were a complete ninny she brings him to the adjoining balcony. He patters across the floor. Having been blissfully parboiled in a small vat, he is no longer pompous. I observe a small bespectacled man with a bulging forehead, a trifle damp, wearing a kimono which is a duplicate of that worn by each gentleman upon the balconies as well as of my own. Before him are set tea-pot and cup, ash-tray combined with a glowing lump of charcoal upon which to light his cigarettes. Madame herself brings his brief-case, and while he speaks is abased in professional humility.

He dines. Course by course, the meal comes from a restaurant upon the head of a liveried runner and is transferred by the crone from lacquered food boxes to Madame's own costly pottery of which no two pieces are alike, being the original work of master potters. He dines slowly, interminably. He eats, reads thick documents drawn from the brief-case, eats again, reads again. Before he is quite done the two geisha which Madame ordered for him have arrived.

As if inspecting a pair of sawdust dolls, puppets without meaning, she straightens sashes, secures hair ornaments, examines the neck lines of their kimonos to see that they sufficiently reveal admirable napes. Since they are younger than her daughter their exaggerated coiffures scarcely reach her shoulder. With lower lips grotesquely daubed, blackened eye-brows and whitened faces they are as alike as painted Easter eggs. By a pigeon-toed toddling and deliberate swaying, they simulate fragility, moving as if their immature bodies swoon beneath the weight of too much embroidery. The gentleman examines them for a moment, responds impersonally to their prostrations, reads again, eats again,

11

Tea House
Waitress

The Landlady's
daughter
—R.B.—Kyoto—'24

reads, eats. Meanwhile they assume graceful postures, arranging the folds of their garments according to previous instruction and practice, sit expressionless, passive. However, between the heavy lids the bird-like eyes glitter, slyly taking account of every balcony within their vision, flashing almost imperceptible signals to other little ones like themselves.

Oh! The gentleman's wine cup is empty. The diminutives twitter. To the low table, hardly more than an invalid's tray, one waddles upon her knees and with grace remarkable in peasant hands, foredoomed to remain thick and graceless, she holds back the trailing sleeve from a thick round arm, and pours the wine. A wife could be no more solicitous. Done at last with food, with documents, he turns to scrutinize his toys. Alack! Upon the eyelid of the first there is the imperceptible threat of a sty! The mouth of the second is badly roughed, being too narrow! Bird-like eyes exchange glittering signals. While the former depicts abjection, bending like a wind-buffeted flower, the latter paints upon her whitened face a mouth with exaggerated lower lip which better suits this middle-aged connoisseur.

To a duet of twitters and squeaks the mature masculine voice responds steadily in a tea-house antiphony. Gossip of geisha life is, I am sure, being related; for from time to time he half rises to stare at figures indicated upon distant balconies, learning, very likely, the name of this month's favorite, or of some lucky beauty whose lover is willing to end by purchase her period of bondage.

The maid brings a long-necked native guitar. But her childish arms are so short that the player to reach the pegs must rest the instrument's body beside her upon the floor and not upon her knee like an adult artist. With a flat piece of ivory she scrapes the strings. After a half-dozen desultory chords, proving her talent, she lays the guitar aside.

Singing as if to herself, the other small one opens and shuts a half-sized fan, twirling it upon her fingertips so that it flutters, a giant butterfly, about the twinkling hair-ornaments, the oiled hair, glossy as black lacquer, her body in its flower-colored kimono. The gentleman appears pleased, incandescent with

12

Wandering
minstrels
sing under
tea-house
balconies

R. B.
Kyoto
1924

winey delight. Through his girdle, thrust like a dagger, he also wears a fan. He performs. Barring a few minor misadventures it is good. Twitter and giggle!

Frankly playful the mood has become. A game! Not a serious game such as men play, squatting for hours, moving counters across a checquered board, but a frivolous game of the tea-houses. From the potter and painter, atrocious linguists, I gather somewhat foggily that the opponents attempt to out-guess each other. Two players, facing each other, throw out a hand, apparently calling the gestures simultaneously. Different aspects of the hand having different significance, score accordingly. Therefore, if two fingers, symbolizing scissors, are extended against a flattened hand indicating paper, then scissors win, for obviously paper can be cut by them. If, however, instead of a flattened hand a doubled fist is extended symbolizing stone, then naturally scissors lose. There are apparently dozens, it seems, of these symbols. The game, constantly accelerated, remains rhythmic, having in it the elements of a pantomimic dance, charming even to one who peers at great disadvantage through gaps in a balcony balustrade.

They tire. After a silence one puppet brings out of her sleeve a packet of papers carried by every Japanese, papers which serve innumerable purposes, as napkins, handkerchiefs, tea-cake wrappings. By dexterous folding she makes from these small squares a boat, a flower, a spread-winged bird. But the gentleman himself produces an infinitesimal paper frog! Wondrous amphibian! Triumph of creative art! Twitter and giggle.

All along the river bank is a terrific crashing and slamming. In houses from which the guests are gone, or where they are already abed, maids pull glass panels of river-view rooms into their proper grooves, barring them against nimble prowlers. Long ago the courtesans accompanied the three handsome youths indoors. Dreamily, the potter and the painter watch sparkling plumes of fire wave and disappear above the black river. In this cold light, waders touching off the rockets at the behest of Madame or some other tea-house manager, are momentarily revealed. It is time that potter and artist went home to their young wives. It is time for the little ones to go. This is the unspoken message in

13

Madame's coming. They receive from the gentleman two colored envelopes enclosing small gifts of money for themselves, the fee due their master or mistress being collected from him by Madame. Swaying as if their bodies swooned beneath the weight of silk, they toddle out of view. Tucked into a double rickshaw, alike as two painted Easter eggs, from beneath downcast eyes scanning the passersby, they return to the street across the river.

The gentleman tosses away a half-finished cigarette, patters along the corridor, his night-out at an end.

When I ascend to my river-view room, now become an airless glass and paper box, a short, pompous figure in immaculate tweeds struts towards the gateway between bowing maids. In the entry Madame, the shadow of a school-girl beside her, clutches a handful of paper yen. Until there is no longer any sound of the motor she kneels in professional humility.

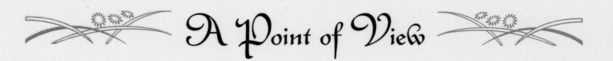

A Point of View

THROUGHOUT this old temple, throughout its courtyards in which aged pines spread twisted branches, and its enclosed gardens in which lotus buds rising above steamy pools fall open silently, there breathes a sweet and drowsy face. Along open galleries, over handhewn floors darkly stained with the juice of some plant, never touched by shoes, worn satiny by the passage of bare feet, I follow the old painter of Buddhas. An ancestor of his, when the temple was new, painted lotuses, still discernible, upon walls behind two altars. Through rooms we pass, rooms which ceased centuries ago to be large, or small, ceased to be square, when their walls were projected into indefinite space by mural decorators who painted upon them in great sweeping rhythms as fundamental as the rise and fall of the sea. Here I kneel with the old painter, dwarfed by these conceptions, where

14

Even in Tokyo
youth must have
its Quartier Latin,
its Greenwich Village
RB '24

C LeRoy Baldridge
TOKYO - 25

Even the humblest burn incense
before the tablets of the Forty-Seven
Feudal knights who dedicated their
lives to avenging their Master

believers, intellectuals, aristocratic warriors, once knelt. Then as now throbbed through their reveries a drumming, primitive and yet, being unaccented, escaping savagery, a monotonous reiteration intensifying the peace.

Seated beside the base of a wooden pillar, as beside a tree, a Buddhist nun beats upon a carved wooden drum resembling an enormous over-ripe fruit. She is like an image, eyelids drooping, full-lipped mouth in a fixed sensuous smile, head close-shaven, the ear-lobes artificially elongated by persistent rubbing and pulling. From dwelling within temples and walled gardens she is pale. Having replaced a nun or priest, she in turn will be replaced; and so flows the throbbing out of an ardent past into an indifferent present and, beat by beat, even as I listen, into the future of which none may know. But for me the sweet and drowsy peace is dissipated, the spell which had gently captured me is sundered.

I am to go swimming. With pantomime, vivid, unmistakable, with a few words of understandable English supported by small red-backed dictionaries, the painter and potter, son and protégé of the old man, make this announcement. Where am I to swim? Kyoto is an inland city and the river so low that fishermen wade from shore to shore. I learn nothing more than the place is beautiful, beautiful, beautiful. The two are incoherent, rhapsodic. I make an effort to look pleased, but find no pleasure now in the tea and cakes upon which the temple's crest was imprinted before baking, sent to us by the head priest of the order.

My elderly host, unconcerned with swimming, returns to his tranquil garden, his hot-houses where flowers bloom before their time, and grapes, delicate as glass bubbles, are ripened out of season. And the four of us, the painter, the potter, my husband and I, crowd into a small shop near the temple gate; for if I am to swim, I must have a bathing-suit. Wedged between piles of merchandise, peering through dangling kimonos, sashes, neckties we watch the shopkeeper produce a suit designed for a Japanese lady. Held before me, it scarcely covers my chest, a small black bib. Others are smaller. Busily rooting, the merchant brings out two garments of knitted white cotton, underwear for a fat Japanese gentleman. At least these are wide enough. To carry them I buy one of

16

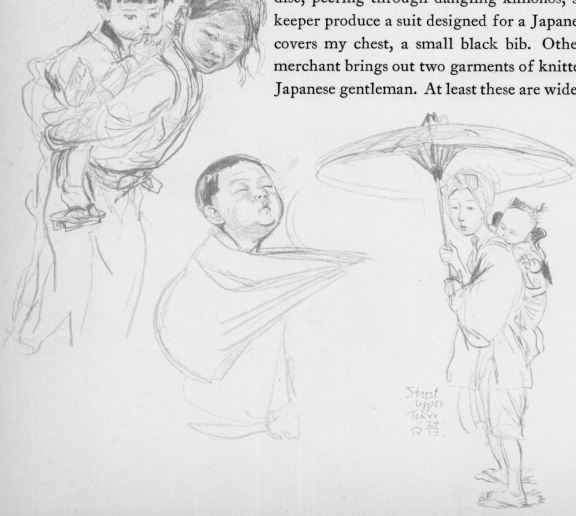

Street types
Tokyo
24
R 13.

Where Chinese Buddhism first
flowered in Japan

CLeRoy Baldridge
NARA
-1925

those handkerchiefs for the purpose upon which a large grey fish amid dun-colored spume leaps from a poisonously purple sea.

Well outside of the city we leave the trolley car, and entering a copse follow a pathway lined with crumbling ancestral tablets. We come upon no lake, no river! Oh! We are not to swim but to dine. Entirely hidden by trees is a small restaurant. From a corner room upon the second floor nothing is visible except feathery plumes of trees and close by a bamboo grove filled with an eternal twilight, forever resisting the sun. There is no sound except homely kitchen noises and shrilling of crickets so brassy that after a while I am uncertain whether I hear insects or nerves offended by such insistence are vibrating sharply within my ears.

Setting before us a snowdrift of shaved ice and powdered sugar in which are buried rosy cubes of watermelon and round golden fruit, the mistress goes away to arrange for the plucking of two young chickens. In time the maid, a squat peasant, comes, and with long brass chopsticks fills the brazier set into the table's center with hot coals from another which she carries. Over the former in one pan she cooks chopped onion tops, spicy greens, thread-like noodles, cubes of bean curd with the chickens which have been thinly sliced, setting aside the whitest of the flesh to be eaten raw. Repressing a shudder, I argue with myself, reasoning that raw chicken is no more barbarous than oysters and clams, not only raw but feebly palpitating. Moreover, why should I be distressed by raw chicken when I am already filled with disturbing apprehensions? I am to swim. Where? I do not know. Under what conditions? I can not discover. Recklessly I eat the raw chicken; my husband turns away his head, unequal to the sight. Dipped into soy sauce, washed down with saki, it is delicious. I clamor for more. There is also rice to be eaten, kept in a covered lacquered box so that it remains damp and sticky. Thus the Japanese prefer it.

Another short ride, the trolley carrying us farther away from the city, we arrive at an amusement park with postal-cards, curios, and celluloid toys for sale. The tea-houses, of the commonest sort, have platforms covered with red

18

Overlooking the Forbidden City,
upon Peking's only hill, goats graze
where Emperors walked

McRoy Baldwigs
PEKING
- 1925

flannel upon which passers-by lounge. But beyond this tawdriness is a river.
Foaming and crashing it comes through a narrow gorge, then suddenly widens
into a great still pool at the base of a wooded mountain. Untouched anywhere by
sunlight it is the mountain's shadow grown green and limpid, from which a
delicious chill arises slaking overheated bodies. In this green shadow I am to
swim, in this pool already filled with swimmers, several hundred of them.
There is not a woman among them! No woman is in sight except here and there
a girl sitting upon the bank, badly groomed, unmistakably coarse.

Bath-houses? Observing two buildings, I rush towards them, followed by
painter and potter, their wooden clogs rattling over the rocky trail. These are
tea-houses, not bath-houses, filled with men, smoking, talking. There are no
other buildings. Frantically I scan the landscape until my predicament is under-
stood. I look for a proper place in which to strip off my clothing. To a row of
platforms where elderly custodians guard the neatly piled garments of the
swimmers, I am led. Here in plain view of the tea-houses, of the swimmers, of
Japan, I am expected to undress. I can not. I will not. But the mountain is so
steep that I can not take shelter behind a pine tree. The opposite bank, equally
precipitous, is barren and sunlit. Meanwhile, slowly, irresistibly, as if magne-
tized, the swimmers turn in their courses and hundreds of black heads bob like
corks in the water at my feet.

For me this excursion was arranged. Painter and potter, unable to swim, have
chosen niches in an enormous boulder and expect to sleep. As I stand irresolute,
an unhappy, a baffled look passes between them. If I refuse to swim they will be
distressed. To explain my desire for shelter requires a definition of Western
modesty, an explanation of the Western point of view with reference to the
nude, and a discussion of the probable results of exposure. But these matters can
not be made clear in their poverty-stricken English vocabulary, supported by
pantomime and dictionaries. It occurs to me that empowered by the gift of
tongues I might not be able to make these things clear, accounting also for the
predominance of the human body in Western art, with which these two are

19

Nara—to which
pilgrims come
by tens of thousand
each year

R.B. '25

already familiar, a predominance conspicuously lacking from their own art. Moreover, I do not know what curious, morbid, even monstrous trains of thought may be awakened in these minds if I refuse to undress. For more than one reason this excursion must proceed. Feigning delight I point to the opposite bank, that at least is uninhabited. And while my two companions curl into their niches my husband rows with me to the opposite shore, the purple bundle resting upon my trembling knees. The swimmers' black heads, irresistibly drawn, wheel, moving with the boat.

Turning my back upon the pool I feel that I establish some privacy. With difficulty I take off shoes and stockings, balancing precariously among sharp rocks and mud-holes. My dress I pull over my head with one motion so that I am scantily covered by the simplest of lingerie. My hands, numb with nervousness, are nearly useless and I must rest. Behind me the swimmers gurgle, splash. What do they await? Too well I know. They await that horrible, that never-to-be-survived moment when I stand before them, the largest and most undressed woman in the whole universe; and they will jeer, cat-call, howl me down.

I spread out the two ridiculous pieces of underwear. Relying now upon speed to confound my observers I rip off the balance of my covering with motions up and motions down. The horrible moment over, I stand clothed in the absurd knit garments. But the outburst! I listen. Splashing, gurgling, the swimmers otherwise remain silent. Slowly I turn about and, facing them, slip into the mountain's shadow, sink my conspicuous whiteness into the deep green. Hand over hand I pull myself through the water accompanied by the swimmers. The foreign woman swims! They wax garrulous. For this demonstration and this alone they waited. When I tire a skiff is loaned. Clambering into it I discover that the underwear, already brief, is shrinking, that wet, it is transparent. But nobody seems to see or care. And so long as nobody cares, my caring becomes pointless, silly.

Nobody cares, least of all myself.

20

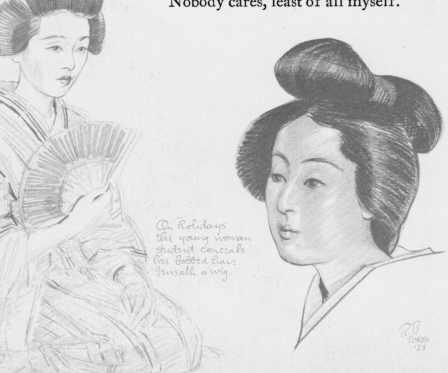

On holidays
the young woman
student conceals
her bobbed hair
beneath a wig.

One Little Gesture

SATURATED with exclusiveness, cloying as fumes in a confectioner's kitchen, is this atmosphere. The open stage, actors' runway at the left, raised square covered with padded mats for the audience, lie within a low wall of seamless cloth, dazzling white, and striped vertically with cleanly black. Beyond this barrier, where a pathway ends upon high ground before a sudden descent by stairway, the heads of holiday makers pass; those of men close-shaven for the summer, those of women balancing complicated coiffures, glossy black hair drawn over hidden framework. Drolly small behind these adult heads are those of babes riding upon the backs of parents. This being by Royal Decree a holiday, simple folk, workers, keepers of small shops, visit the Thunder God's shrine, and by paying their nationalistic respects to this Imperial ancestor honor their ruler. As one after another of the hundreds tweaks the bell-rope a flat-toned, almost toneless gong jangles incessantly.

Guarding their secrets of technique like members of a mystic cult, actors once played upon this ancient stage before nobles and minor aristocrats. Well-born young men of artistic temperament, trained by a professional, present Nō dramas before well-born relatives, the drama's modern patrons, aristocrats of an industrial age among whom are descendants of the noble class. This audience, kneeling upon the raised square, is low-keyed and discreet. Women converse and titter behind spread fans. Ceremoniously the right people bow, and are bowed to by the right people. Following upon each arrival the audience is freshly swept to the floor in a gust of bowing. The manner of summoning or rebuking ushers who distribute hot tea, ash receivers, or ices is faultless in its superiority. The kimonos, except those of young women, are of rich, dark silk and, upon many, crests are conspicuous. One man only, sitting nearby, scribbling in a note-book, wears foreign dress. Out-of-fashion and quaintly too large are his faded brown suit and the flapping hat which once were matched. So that dust will not be tracked

21

upon the immaculate matting hideous flannel bags were pulled over his shoes by the door-tender. These bags, horrible, monstrous—I abandoned my shoes at the entrance, believing my mind weakly incapable of resisting their clumsy, muffling, generally irritating effect.

To savor this special atmosphere I come, expecting nothing from the drama, although not entirely ignorant of it. In the past I have heard people who read English translations, who attended modified performances in America by Japanese long absent from Japan, talk of it charmingly, convincingly. They described the action as set in a shadowy margin of reality, this unreality sustained by male masked actors upon a barren stage, using no properties except now and then something skeletonized into a symbol stimulating the spectator's imagination. This would be difficult to follow; but I said that I must, indeed, I must see such a performance! But a Japanese has since whispered that classical examples of these plays of unknown origin, in phraseology obscure, remain incomprehensible to any but over-alert intellectuals. I observe the audience bends intently above wide-open books, explanations of the plays. Anyway, there is atmosphere.

Against the background of natural wood across which a sprawling branch of pine is painted, the musicians arrange themselves, a grave and solemn row with bamboo flutes, and tasselled drums shaped like hour-glasses. The music, either without singing quality, or with measures too unfamiliarly long, seems to have no rhythm. While one man chants, the drums give off sounds unlike drumming but akin to wood struck by wood. There are repeated cries as of a sleeper who dreams of screaming but can not wake and makes choking, unearthly cries in the darkness, cries inseparable from terror and a world beyond the listener's reach.

Into my hand the note-book is pressed by the man in seedy brown clothes. He has written a meager description of the play. The curly, ornate capitals, the cramped slanting letters, belong to the period of his wardrobe's prime. The story, he writes, is that of a Second Wife, meaning a concubine, famous for virtuous loyalty to her master, a shogun, and to her mother, who, lying ill in another village, begs her daughter to return.

22

Barter Everywhere —
in ancient shops and
transient sidewalk
markets —

C·LeRoy Baldridge
PEKING -24

The shogun enters, wearing a costume of dark stuff, his face unmasked. Seated upon a mat he speaks, and speaks, and speaks, his voice rising and falling uninfluenced by the music, which continues. There is nothing here to please the eye. The audience bends over its books. By half-turning I can watch the doorway of the shrine where two young men, garlands about their necks, flowers upon ludicrous peasant hats, cling like drowning men to the bell-rope rattling the tinny gong. A winey unsteadiness of feet keeps them at it indefinitely. But from this comedy I am withdrawn by the urgent nudging of the little man.

At last the shogun is silent. Through the curtained runway of the actors comes another figure, proceeding with inhuman steadiness, with inhuman slowness, as if drawn along a track by invisible wires. The kimono, scarlet, gold and white brocade, conceals the figure which it covers. Jetty black hair falls like a hood upon either side of a round white moon face, a mask. Through slits for eyes, no eyes are visible. A silly, simpering mouth is carved upon it. One hand clasps a fan, the other a scroll, the mother's letter. This then is the Second Wife.

Without change except in direction, wheeling, gliding, the mask, the wig, the stuffed kimono approach the shogun. From the mask, echoing in the rounded spaces behind the cheeks comes a voice as from afar. Accepting the letter the shogun reads aloud, speaks, speaks, his droning voice now the only sound except the gong's faint clatter, the figure standing before him woodenly, stiff fingers curled about the fan.

And then suddenly I am filled with indescribable pain. One slow gesture has wounded me beyond belief, one slow gesture, sharp as a cry in the silence—the first gesture, the only gesture. Hard, cruelly hard, the doll has pressed against its mouth the tip of the folded fan. Against the carved and painted simpering lips of a moon-faced mask a fan is pressed. But in that moment a doll, coming to life, lives the whole span of an Oriental woman's existence, sorrows with a pent-up intensity from which I can never altogether recover. Always and forever that gesture is to remain with me.

Stunned, I am only dimly aware of what follows. The shogun apparently

23

relents his formal refusal. Into the white outlines of a boat, a sketch in slender strips of wood, the mannequin glides and, lifting the outlines slowly, slowly sails away with it, sails down the actors' runway, disembarks and is lost behind the actors' curtain.

There will be other plays. The audience dines upon cold rice, rolled and wrapped in sea-weed, served with cold fish in small hand-carved wooden boats. But I come away to watch garlanded revelers in the sunlight, hoping to forget my pain.

Oh, To Be First

A T THE Fox God's shrine in the restaurant garden she leaves a twisted "prayer paper." For a lover, perhaps, the waitress prays? No, she answers the Japanese potter, she has one. Serving done, she lingers, eyes fixed upon mine with curious urgency. What does she want?—To go as my servant to America, enslaved until I free her! And yet here it is almost idyllic, despite small wages which must be eked out by tips from rustic diners. Screened by overhanging branches, built at different levels, open like balconies, the rooms belong to tree-tops and sky. Dappled by shadow patterns is the courtyard. Water vessels clink merrily at the well. There is pagan laughter of housemaids, and of young farmers who for coolness knot about their brows blue cotton towels chilled in well water.

Why would she go? To be first; above all things, to come first! The potter, her superior by birth and sex, is incredulous of what she has heard, that even a kitchen wench need not step aside in America for any man, stranger, relative or friend! To enter a street car first, for this she would cross the ocean. And it is for this the waitress prays.

24

Equally destitute, scholars and
human draft animals live
side by side in mud huts

Dignity of bearing, heritage from
a lost culture, have Korean women
- subjects now of Japan-

C Le Roy Baldridge-
Pyeng -ang -KOREA

The Dancing Girl
Seoul '24

 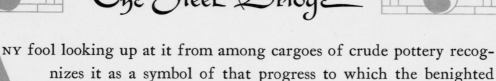 # The Steel Bridge

ANY fool looking up at it from among cargoes of crude pottery recognizes it as a symbol of that progress to which the benighted Koreans are being introduced by their rulers—for their own good, mind you, entirely for their own good and in keeping with precedent. This symbol is a bridge, a steel bridge, spanning the lazy river. You couldn't find a better example of construction anywhere, says the pinkish man, travelling with a show of California products, who visits this mission because a church-going relative in Los Angeles bade him to. It interests him little; but in a government car escorted by a government clerk, as he has been since first his stout American shoes struck upon Korean soil, he looked at the bridge. "You got to hand it to the Japs." I do not care to hear.

Even the missionary is impressed, although he inclines to share with the Koreans a suspicion of innovations. For instance, he could not be expected to welcome the sudden imposition of a foreign tongue upon his converts and pupils, threatening schools and churches with confusion. In Mikado worship he sees, as a Christian evangelist, no improvement upon native animism. With reference to laws and law-making, however, he is more tolerant. He respects law. To arrest a Korean because he has no fly-swatter is, he agrees, carrying law and order to excess, but still a good citizen must swat flies. And who ever heard of a country prospering without laws?

Hard white highways, excellent railways, uniting Japan and Manchuria, these are familiar symbols of that civilization which he has long believed superior. And the steel bridge—true, the Koreans, leading their pack animals, use foot-paths, criss-crossing the land. It seems dull of them not to respect symbols, to resist progress by which in the end, it is said, they will profit. Engineering stirs the simple American soul of the missionary. But I do not wish to see the bridge, and will not, as on other days, go down to the river.

27

Musicians whose business
it is to supply Korean men
with dancing girls-
R.B-SEOUL -24

I do not stand today among the cargoes, glazed pickle jars, any one of which would conceal a full-grown man, and lava-colored water-jars such as women and girls carry upon their heads. I am not there to watch ragged fishermen, peasant women working like draft animals, faces leathery and puckered from the sun, or wooden boats scanning the river with eyes painted upon up-sweeping prows. For me a blur of white falls, falls through darkness, turns, twists, strikes the lazy river, cleaving it, rides for a moment upon the current and is forever gone. Last night from the steel bridge a Korean girl threw herself into the river. Her body was found by fishermen at dawn.

Not much over sixteen, she had been wed to a youth of her own age, wed in the traditional manner, by arrangement between families. Such a marriage being almost inviolable, a divorce would be the affair, not of individuals, but of clans. From the first, the girl was gentle, knowing a wife's duty. But the young man was of a newer mold, a rebel against tradition, against old-fashioned authority. He wished to choose a wife for himself. To the local authorities, the new rulers whose power is naturally greater than that of a subject's father, he went, appealing in the name of a law, as new as the bridge, and as alien. What he demanded was granted—a modern divorce.

She who had been a bride was now neither wife nor yet a maid free to reenter her father's house, eligible again for marriage. No respected Korean family would accept her as daughter-in-law. Scorned publicly by her husband, she was disgraced, and her shame became the shame of her bewildered relatives. In her father's house she was, as in her husband's, unwelcome.

Wearing fresh white linens from her bridal chest, she ran, last night, to meet death. Through stinking streets, past barred gates of unfriendly houses, past barred gates of the mission's gardens, she ran, a whimpering thing in white, while we lay between decent sheets, dreaming.

This is the story which I got this morning from the missionary's wife, whose cook had it from the gatekeeper, he having listened to the gossip of peddlers.

Today I will not go down to the river.

28

Korea P.B. 1919.

Ck Roy Baldridge
on the Great Wall — '25

CkRoy Baldridge PEKING 1924

Encircling walls, though ancient,
breed security in Peking —

Wooden arch
marking
the way
to Confucian Temple

THE very name sings itself—Peking; city of every wanderer's desire. September, the perfect month. No cloud of dust whipped skyward from the plain in whirling columns covers the sun, bathing the city in unholy saffron light, until, the wind's tension ended, it falls, obscuring man from man. No deluge beats upon dirt walls of humblest houses, transforming them into clotted mud, into ooze and slime, seeking again the earth.

Pink walls of palaces, mellowed with age, uphold roofs of Imperial yellow, of jade green, glittering dragons chained astride the ridgepoles. Flame-colored doors, studded with brass, lead through grey walls behind which the domestic life is hid. Through deposits of dust, despite decay, flakes of yellow, blue, green are still apparent upon rotting wooden arches which span old highways. Dimly the gilt still shines upon carved shop-fronts. Red boxes and blue jars stand upon peddlers' trays and in shops. Blue are the canopies of Peking carts, and blue the garments of the multitude. Cotton coolie cloth, blue and clean, soiled, tattered, decently patched but faded to the mauve of a moth's wing, effaces by its profusion the fleeting impressions of dark gowns worn by scholarly gentlemen, and flower-colored jackets of young women.

Distressing, so much color, to my tame eyes.

An ant world! From an inexhaustible font humanity in blue coolie cloth pours, coming at sunrise, making, mending, fetching, carrying; when weary, sleeping beside the road; when hungry, eating. Again it makes, mends, fetches, carries, buys, sells, at sunset going. A man-power world, life's tempo determined by man, there is the effect of race energy deliberately conserved according to some ancient and secret comprehension of man's abilities, conserved for a trek through centuries, across unknowable distances, unconcerned with the arrival of one more pallid foreigner, uninvited, come to exhort, to exploit, to stare—if

31

The Pink Wall
PEKING

surviving—inevitably to depart from Asia. My existence unverified by hostility or even curiosity, the sense of my own being weakens.

I am a shadow wandering in a world of ants!

An excess of sound, preponderantly human, fills me with disquiet. With now and then a plaintive singing cry, hawkers scream, howl, beat upon drums, bang gongs, blow trumpets, calling their wares. In open shops workmen hammer upon tin, brass, copper utensils. Laden with sorrow is the tune played by a blind man upon his flute. There is a continuous whimpering as against their brass basins itinerant barbers strike giant tweezers, obvious emblems of the trade. Wooden hubs grind horribly upon ungreased wooden axles as two-wheeled vehicles of all sorts traverse the city, sounding only a little more horrible than primitive pulleys above public wells. In aged half-dead trees rooks and showy magpies scold, while overhead, low-flying pigeons, with reed whistles fastened upon them, fill the air with wailing.

By stupid fear of the unfamiliar I am undone.

Beneath a brassy sky, the population goes hatless, except a few youths in Western hats and men in visorless Chinese skull-caps. Non-protuberant eyes, identically black, as are the heads of jet black hair, set flatly in faces inclined towards flatness, are protected by drooping, fleshy lids. Old ivory, tawny from sunlight, waxen as magnolia petals, the complexions of smooth, hairless faces are even-colored and without blemish. There is no brilliant shade, cerise, coral pink, kingfisher blue, jade green, which does not become a Chinese woman as jacket or as flower thrust into her hair. Common to both sexes are small quick-moving hands, formed for deftness. Peculiarly civilized hands I see among hawkers, water-purveyors, garbage-carriers, stone-masons, beggars. Men with bodies as beautifully coordinated as those of dancers, men in no Western sense athletes, run between rickshaw shafts, carry balanced upon the ends of limber poles loads too heavy for small pack animals. Man-power, stronger, is more plentiful, cheaper. All that I observe tends to make me aware of being pop-eyed, sharp-featured. My nose, a rather decent one, now sticks out too far. A

32

ROOVES
PEKING
'19

Temple at Summit — Tai-Shan —

The first flight - Tai-shan   ChaRoy Baldridge
-1925-

City Wall
Tai-an-fu

brownish brunette, my complexion is subject to freckles, to sudden transformations caused by weather, sweets, emotion. Drab, blotchy, I feel, and also piqued; for not yet have I seen a color that I would venture to wear. My hands, large and useful, now offend me.

A conviction of the physical ineptitude of all my kind depresses me.

Almost under foot food hawkers with giant teakettles and portable stoves ply their restaurant trade along the streets, selling coarse breads, noodles, stewed cabbage, sliced raw radishes, savory soups of mushrooms and garlic, bean-curd with now and then a tidbit of cooked meat. By some miracle of assimilation this diet sustains those whose manual labor is most exhausting. Repeatedly, dust spurting from beneath the feet of men and animals, from beneath the wheels of rickshaws and carts, envelops cooks and patrons, falls into open tureens. From bowls streaked with leavings of other meals, often many times mended with brass rivets, the food is eaten. Some strange immunity these diners possess. Appetites are unaffected by sore-covered pariah dogs nosing for filth, by sewage in baskets upon hand-barrows wheeled slowly by. And yet I am certain that I must have eggs, cereals, meat, and milk, or collapse. For me, an Anglo-Saxon, disease lurks in this dust with which throat and nostrils already tingle. There is disease and death in raw and undercooked food, handled by unwashed Oriental hands, served upon unclean dishes. The thought of eating under such conditions is nauseous.

Ah me! I never felt more finicky, more frail.

No margin of waste is apparent. Foodstuffs in unbelievably small quantities are bought by women and children. Pellets of coal dust molded with clay, only a few bought at a time, are common as fuel. Garments, threadbare and patched, are again patched by a very old woman, squatting in a doorway. A wayside cobbler cuts new soles from discarded rubber tires, from thick sheets made of innumerable layers of cast-off cloth and paper, one layer pasted upon another. Exhibited for sale are pitiful collections of tin cans, bottles, bits of wire, lead, leather. In a basket strapped upon her crooked back, a middle-aged woman collects infinitesimal scraps of paper and cloth. Crawling over dumps, adults and

34

C. LeRoy Baldridge— NANKING /25

Looted in successive revolutions,
restored by foreignized associations,
there remains to this ancient
seat of culture little of its
original beauty.

children salvage pieces of charcoal, clinkers, to be used again. Beggars and dogs garner and eat unspeakable fragments of food. And yet these people are to my fancy endowed with dignity, except the whining beggars, possessed of uncanny vitality, running at my side. Ragged men, meeting, bow aristocratically. Ragged women, neatly groomed, go on their way, a well-bred reserve in every gesture. And there is laughter, neither loud nor boisterous, but smiling, easy, persistent, as if souls fed upon some special philosophy survived, without irritability, misery, degradation, an economic struggle, not only merciless but almost indecently exposed, standards of living unbelievably low, labor unspeakably menial. Above all things this laughter baffles me. Truly, I am a stranger here.

In impressions received so quickly that they overrun there is something painful. Shrinking from the experience's intensity, I am filled with panic. Homesick, in the hotel-room's complete repudiation of the Orient, every stick of furniture being blatantly Occidental, I find comfort. At the door, China howls, screams, beats upon brass, upon copper. But fastening my eyes upon a framed tapestry square, hung askew, my confidence is somewhat restored. Emerging from a dog-kennel upon all fours, the child depicted by this treasure of Central European machine-art is unmistakably a Nordic blonde!

"One little, two little wives—"

BEFORE me in the darkness runs the rickshaw coolie, feet thudding upon frozen ground. Noiselessly the wheels of the rickshaw revolve. Around corners and around corners he runs, through dim crooked streets, between high windowless walls of residence compounds, passing closed gates shadowed by over-hanging tiled porticoes, passing shop-fronts illumined from within so that patterns of carved wood, fretwork of bats and peonies are blackly silhouetted upon paper windows. Scrawled over with red and black characters, paper lanterns hung above shop-

35

There arises the wailing and
strumming of blind minstrels—

R B
PEKING
'25

doors tremble, swayed by some imperceptible breath of the winter night. Dull stars against the starlit sky, small lanterns are lashed to poles above certain house-tops and mark bath-house entrances. Into the street where lives the old scholar with his two wives the rickshaw silently spins. From a pavilion adjoining the gate arises the wailing, strumming, and drumming of blind minstrels; for this evening there is to be feasting. Beneath the rickshaw coolie's hands brass knockers jangle. Within, bolts are noisily drawn. The gates swing open. I step over the high sill, and behind me the gates are again noisily barred.

Beside his young wife, whose flesh is creamy and whose eyes are somnolent, the old scholar appears small and brittle. Obviously the plump young woman is delighted with the rôle of hostess. She bustles importantly, stirring without result the fire in a sullen, undersized stove. Her hands, exquisite from idleness, beckon the guests to chairs. She drops fresh powdered incense upon glowing charcoal in a bronze brazier. And in everything is she prettily assisted by the concubine, a delicately fading beauty, and Moon Flower, the pert young daughter of the concubine who is half the age of her mother and almost as old as her father's Number One Wife.

In the arms of a nurse the first child of the Number One Wife, an infant daughter, is brought in; she howls and grows convulsive at the sight of foreigners. Unobtrusively three boys present themselves. They are brothers. The eldest is a person of consequence because he is the household's First Born; also he goes to school in Shanghai and is at home only for the New Year's prolonged festivities. He is almost of an age with Moon Flower and, like her, little younger than his father's young wife. The youngest boy is young enough to be treated as a doll, lifted from lap to lap. He wears colored silks, and cocked ludicrously upon his head is a rakish crocheted hat of his own choosing, designed for some school-girl in the foreign quarter. The eldest is so important and the youngest so winning that the middle boy, a frail-looking lad, is overlooked and slips away to the other pavilion so that he can stand close beside the fat minstrel as if seeking warmth for his thin body.

36

The concubine is
young and plump,
the Number 2 wife
of delicately fading
Beauty

R.B
PEKING
-25-

Their story I am told by a foreign guest. When the eldest boy and Moon Flower were both infants their mothers, themselves girls, lived together in peace beneath the roof of the scholar, then a middle-aged provincial official. But peace was dissipated when the boys' mother, the Number One Wife, came under the influence of American missionaries. As a Christian converted to an alien religion of love she became relentlessly monogamistic and thrust out of her house the concubine with her infant Moon Flower. Mother and child suffered miserably in a society which offers no refuge to a foot-loose woman. That this tragedy was to some extent secretly relieved by the husband is certain. After the birth of the third boy this Number One Wife died and the widower then called upon the concubine to return with Moon Flower so that she could care for the sons as if they were her own. This she did and remains in the household, their devoted foster-mother, a willing subordinate to the young Number One Wife, and as the Number Two Wife of the old scholar.

Slowly and in no particular direction Oriental pleasure proceeds. Before dawn there will be a feast. In some angle between out-building and compound wall an itinerant caterer has set up his portable stove, for from this obscure corner come sounds of sizzling grease, of cold water poured into hot iron kettles. When a stove-hole is uncovered a coppery light momentarily inflames the square inner courtyard, flanked on four sides by detached residence pavilions, and it reveals for that instant eaves and beam-ends decorated with pictures in red, green and blue. To the feast the caterer, it is promised, will send among other things sharks' lips and gills of an astonishing sliminess, palatable but almost impossible to impinge between the silver points of red bone chopsticks.

Already slow, the tempo of the evening is further retarded. For conversation must pass as through a mesh, through the differently attuned personalities of a foreigner who speaks Mandarin and a Chinese whose English is pedantic.

Tea is served, pale tea in small bowls. By combined efforts the three women succeed in propelling forward a servant who sets upon the table a platter of French pastry, well lathered with whipped canned milk. About this platter the

37

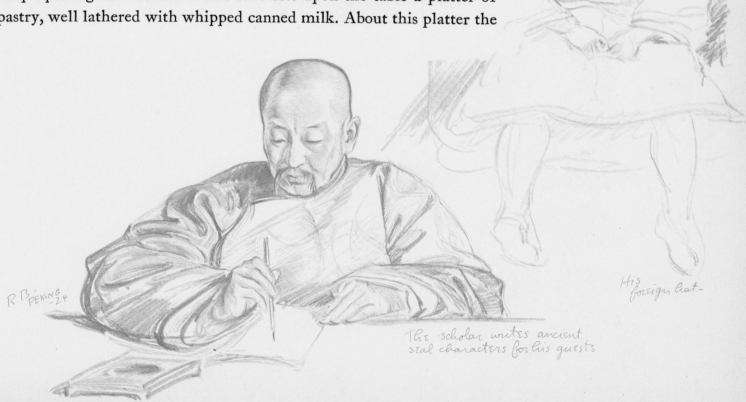

His foreign hat.

The scholar writes ancient seal characters for his guests

youngest boy bobs, in his eagerness tumbling over the feet of his elders, hoisting himself to their knees for a better view and shorter reach. His insatiability becomes a diversion. When the empty platter is carried away it is replaced by dishes of roasted water-melon seeds, shelled peanuts and dried dates. Crackling, crumbling, nibbling follows and a fine sawdust of discarded hulls collects upon knees and chests. After a time these dishes are replenished and taken to the pavilion where the four blind minstrels strum, drum and wail. Now and again a winging melody floats like a ragged ribbon but is lost again in the din of brasses. Under cover of the racket Moon Flower becomes confidential.

A spirited little thing in stiff green silk coat and trousers she is. Against her oiled black hair she has set an artificial flower of brilliant pink. She does not wear, as do the adults, layer upon layer of garments padded with silk waste or lined with fur, perfect insulation against the icy needles of cold which press in through every pore of a Chinese house. But like them she wears foreign bedroom slippers of felt, these being the only protection against the graveyard chill of stone floors. She shows me that like any other flapper she rolls her stockings below bare knees.

A charming idle hand is extended so that I may admire her one ring, dark green jade set in gold, a gift from her father. I examine the concubine's ring, of which the stone is larger and clearer. The young wife puts forth her hand so that I admire hers, which is the finest, a large, pale green stone surrounded by small diamonds. That these marked differences in value are proper Moon Flower makes known to me by pantomime and in broken English from some remote school-day. The wife she indicates as "Number One," her mother as "Number Two," and as for herself, she makes a gesture of humility. I understand that she is of no particular importance.

The feast! A flurry of husks and sawdust brushed from chests and knees follows the summons. Through the bitter chill of the inner courtyard the old scholar leads the way to the dining room where a round dining-table, hired for the occasion, is covered with a coarse white cotton cloth. From the caterer's stove

38

Novices
"Bridge of Heaven
Tea House"
PEKING P.B: 2⁵

outside banners of coppery light are flung against the dining-room window. A
door is opened dramatically and three servants enter bearing enormous bowls
from which the steam rises and beclouds the room. There is a stew of fish and
shrimps, shell fish brought from the sea-coast many miles away, a stew of spiced
chicken and a kidney stew. Warm rice wine is poured into small porcelain bowls.
The food is savory beyond description. Moon Flower and her mother eat sparingly with what seems to be an affectation of daintiness. But having had no
experience in these matters except an occasional meal of Occidental proportions
in the Chinatowns of San Francisco and New York, and in a much gilded Oriental café of Paris, I assume that these three bowls are the feast and eat shame-
lessly. With longing the Number One Wife watches from beneath sleepy eyelids, for as the wife of a Buddhist she has become a vegetarian and shares the
herbs and eggs set before her husband. The foreign brandy, which he drinks like
water from a tall goblet, she refuses.

Away go the three bowls. Birds' nest soup, sharks' lips and gills, boiled greens
follow with balls of hot coarse bread. One ball is four times the size of a baking
powder biscuit but far more delicious than any biscuit or dumpling, which it
somewhat resembles. The porcelain cups are filled to the brim with warm wine.
Moon Flower and her mother pluck sparingly at the food. Herbs and eggs in
another style are placed before the host and his wife. His goblet is refilled.
Another portion of food, another bowl of wine and death from over-eating is
for me inevitable. But the feast must be at an end. I discover sweets in some of
the bread-balls which I fancy may be the dessert. My hand aches from manip-
ulating chop-sticks. I long for a soft chair and coffee, very black. Again the
table is cleared and there is set upon it a whole duck, a Peking duck, the most
kingly dish in China. With it comes dark red pepper sauce, almost a paste, and
wafers of freshly baked bread, paper-thin like pancakes and unleavened. Each
person dips the pieces of flesh torn from the bird first into the sauce and then
wraps each bit with a wafer. For this moment Moon Flower and her mother
saved their energy. I can only look on while they eat heartily. Gustily the Chi-

39

nese guests belch, for a silent guest is lacking in the refinements of appreciation. I groan silently, filled with regrets. I regret my gluttony. As I look at the duck I regret the three stews, the soup, the shark, especially the balls of bread. Once more the table is cleared for an enormous soupy stew of sea-slugs and small onions.

I am become a gorged python. So enveloped in lethargy am I that my sight fails. Either I am falling asleep or am hypnotized by the brutally high-powered electric light, hung Chinese fashion level with the eyes and unshaded, above the center of the table. I perceive, although dimly, that the old scholar is telling a long tale. Intrigued, the women lean towards him. When he has finished they smile at each other and smile at him. In turn he smiles widely, perhaps a trifle alcoholically, upon them and upon his guests encircling the round table and the cotton tablecloth, now criss-crossed with pathways of dripping and food-spots. He drains his goblet, rises and through the revivifying cold of the courtyard returns to the reception room.

The story comes to me at last, filtered through the personalities of the two interpreters. Long, long ago, before this Number One Wife, the eldest son, and Moon Flower were born, long before the mother of the three boys had become his wife, and before he had ever set eyes upon his concubine, there had been still another Number One Wife, the bride of his early youth, who had lived with him and died, leaving no children. In all the many years since her death he had never found in another Chinese woman such beauty, such culture and wisdom. When few knew English, she spoke it fluently. Her father, an official, had educated her as a boy is educated in China. When he became a diplomat despatched by the Imperial Government to London he had taken with him this daughter. Upon this trip she was presented at the court of Queen Victoria. My face is searched by the scholar and the three women. I, too, am touched on this night by the honor with which Queen Victoria's court and the memory of that Number One Wife still envelop this Peking household.

Towards dawn the evening ambles. There are things to enjoy through the fingertips and eyes, and through the eyes alone. From glass boxes and out of

40

silken bags the women withdraw a variety of baubles, seals carved out of semi-precious stone, a wonderful white jade, statuettes of legendary folk carved out of tea root. Upon the red wall of the reception room a picture is unrolled. It is a Ming painting of a bird upon a branch. Its curving tail forms a pattern over more than half the length of the narrow panel. While the silk is yellowed the blue paint, made from ground lapis, is singularly brilliant.

Upon a carved ink-slab the scholar mixes his ink and, moistening a brush, writes upon thin strips of paper the ancient seal characters. For this accomplishment, which is becoming rare, he is famous. Even to my untrained eye this picture-writing becomes significant and exceedingly beautiful. A fish, a bird, a tree, a house, a drum, falling rain, rising sun, the moon, these recognizable objects are symbols of phrases. Upon the scholar's desk is an ivory receptacle shaped like a tall glass and filled with ivory sticks upon which are etched inscriptions. This was the plaything of nobles two hundred years ago and is similar to the bamboo holder from which the street-corner astrologer shakes a bamboo stick upon which is inscribed the fate of his client. It was once customary for a host to rattle the sticks in their ivory cup, throwing one out upon the table as dice are shaken and thrown. And the inscription in those bibulous days determined for whom the next drink was to be poured. Upon one is written that the brothers must drink together, upon another that the eldest must drink, likewise the youngest, the two who have most recently met, the first to arrive, or the one who has travelled farthest to the feast. Thus no princely guest escapes.

Against another powerful electric light the old scholar raises a white porcelain cup, in texture and design a half-opened lotus flower in the center of which stands a diminutive porcelain man with the garments of a sage. Filled to the level of the figure's shoulders the cup behaves as any other cup, but when the little man is drowned the entire contents suddenly dribbles mysteriously from beneath him so that the drinker is thoroughly wet. Over this mischievous warning to the intemperate of two hundred years ago the women giggle, politely holding their sleeves over their mouths.

41

Shanghai
- 1919 -

As a gracious dismissal the old scholar makes a gift of the cup. Across the courtyard the itinerant caterer has long since passed with kettles and stove slung from the ends of his limber carrying pole. From the pavilion adjoining the gate house there is no longer any sound, for the blind minstrels, aided by the servants, are feasting. The old scholar waves a thin hand with finger-nails extending far beyond finger-tips towards a scroll upon the wall. Half-singing, half-reciting, he reads what is upon it. "It is not my house that matters but the spirit within it." Close about the master of the household the three women gather. In the foreign manner hands touch hands in farewell. For the ghost of a moment an intangible communication exists between the women and myself as their finger-tips linger upon my arms, my wrists, my hands.

Beneath a grey sky from which the stars have receded, down crooked streets, around corners, passing barred gates, passing shops no longer illumined from within, through a grey and sleeping city runs the rickshaw coolie, his feet thudding upon the frozen ground.

The Old Sinner

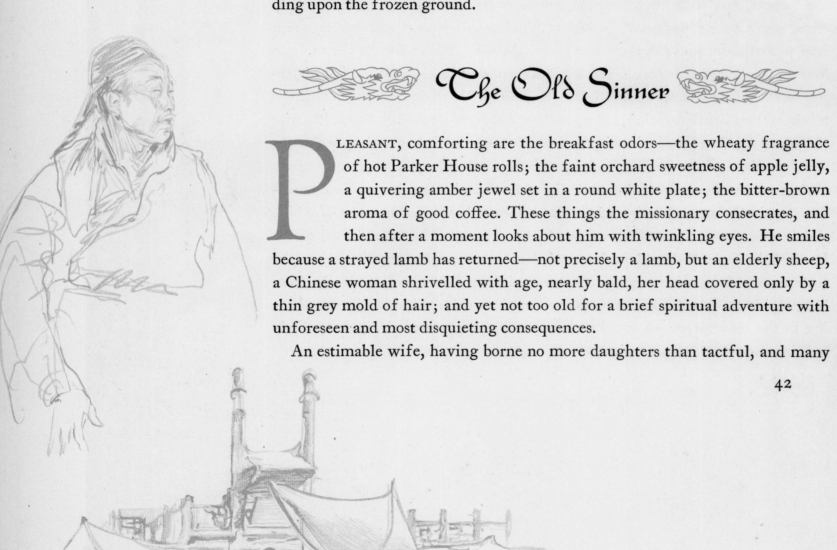

PLEASANT, comforting are the breakfast odors—the wheaty fragrance of hot Parker House rolls; the faint orchard sweetness of apple jelly, a quivering amber jewel set in a round white plate; the bitter-brown aroma of good coffee. These things the missionary consecrates, and then after a moment looks about him with twinkling eyes. He smiles because a strayed lamb has returned—not precisely a lamb, but an elderly sheep, a Chinese woman shrivelled with age, nearly bald, her head covered only by a thin grey mold of hair; and yet not too old for a brief spiritual adventure with unforeseen and most disquieting consequences.

An estimable wife, having borne no more daughters than tactful, and many

42

THE PEKING CART
-R-B-

As the October sun drops behind
the city walls Peking is touched
with a pale and chill enchantment

— C LeRoy Baldridge PEKING - 1924

sons; a good mother, having sent every daughter away to some prospering home a bride, and chosen for each son a wife so competent that her house has no need for servants, she long since retired from all activities except the autocratic government of her daughters-in-law and their innumerable children. This paragon, this self-satisfied old lady, discovered herself to be, in the estimation of a newly arrived American missionary, no better than one of those women whose photographs adorn the public walls of houses visited only by men, or one of those sing-song girls whose beguiling eyes and painted faces are seen through windows of costly sedan chairs, whose raucous singing rises above the din of men feasting. By this stranger she was denounced as an adulteress!

This was disquieting, for in addition to possessing Chinese virtues she considered herself to be something of a Christian, a foreign-style church member. True, she had not sought salvation but had submitted to it gracefully, rather in the spirit of fine courtesy, although there were also practical advantages. Conversion followed upon the cure by foreign doctors of her First Born male grandchild. This precious, this darling, who after her death will light incense and candles, will lay out food upon the altar of her memory, developed a disease common in the community, covering his small head with a cap of noxious sores. Becoming impatient with the slow magic of the native herb doctor, she brought the child, somewhat timidly, to the foreigners' free dispensary. The cure was miraculous. And, therefore, when pressed to become a Christian, she graciously consented, learned what was necessary for a church member to know and professed her new faith publicly. After all, she had many grandchildren, and illnesses were inevitable.

And because she was known to be a convert, the newly arrived missionary sought her out. The leader of a proselyting sect from America, this Man of God had upon his arrival been politely urged by other Men of God to carry the Word elsewhere to inland areas where it had not yet been carried and where foreign predecessors, some of them at the cost of their lives, had not already conquered living conditions, reducing to a minimum both discomfort and danger. He

43

The bridal chair
R.J. PEKING

would not go. The benighted upon the far frontiers were in less jeopardy than those closer by who had been given the Word improperly by Presbyterians, Methodists, Baptists, to say nothing of the Catholics. With these pitiful ones he would stay. Thereupon he begged the old lady to attend his meetings. They were good theatre after the circumspect sessions with which she was familiar.

So that the missionary might ascertain the state of her soul and decide upon her fitness for Paradise, she was asked to lay bare her life. This she did, it being not extraordinary in China. When the simple tale was done the preacher rolled his eyes skyward. He thumped the floor. He groaned with grief. She was, he said, a wicked old sinner, one of the worst, and unless she repented, unless she expiated her sin, his Lord would not permit one of her bound feet to be set within the pearly gates of Heaven.

She was living in sin, this respectable old lady. Thus had she lived for so long that virtue was unknown to her. In her girlhood, when she had reached the age of restlessness and silliness, her family had, as is the custom, wed her to a stranger of their choice, by agreement with his elders. This ceremony, scarcely to be confused with a sacrament, was followed by an unhappy revelation. The groom did not desire his bride. In fact, he would not keep her, being already too poor, burdened beyond his capacities with dependent and aged relatives. However, he was not without a plan. In the village there was a young man of well-to-do parents shopping about everywhere for a comely young woman with which to replace a wife recently deceased. He would, if pleased, pay cash. If the bride would consent to such an arrangement then she would secure a good home, console a widower, bring happiness to the groom's aged relatives through the payment of his debts. Being Chinese and therefore apparently unafraid of economic facts, she agreed to the sale of herself. After the transaction she never again saw her husband, in time coming away from the village, from the province, with her purchaser, as his wife. So devoted did they become that as the husband grew rich he did not clutter up the household with concubines. And now this old lady discovered that her contentment was sinful, her peaceful life wicked.

44

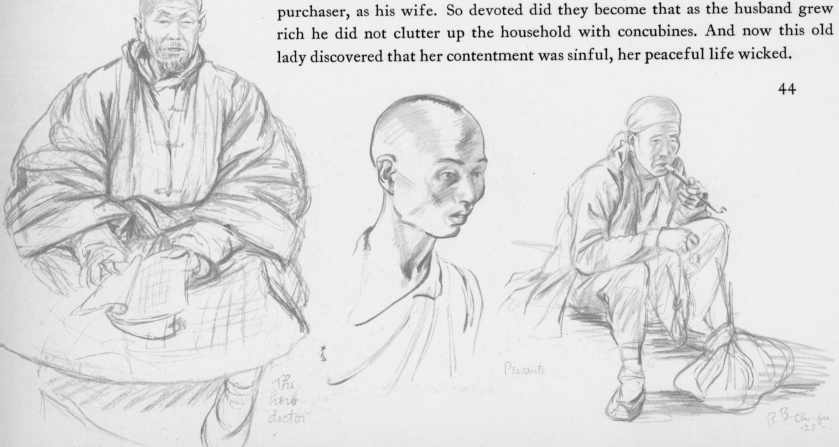

The herb doctor

Peasants

R. B. Chü-fu
-25-

She was extremely disconcerted, not because her hope of a Chinese eternity was affected, the entrance requirements being lax, but since becoming a Christian she had toyed pleasantly with the idea of being eligible as well to a first-class foreign hereafter. Certain of the Chinese eternity in which she would find bolts of silk, servants, thermos bottles, having herself, from time to time, upon birthdays, already burned paper effigies of these useful articles, she did not like to relinquish the idea of visiting, when she desired, a good foreign Heaven. Having foolishly attached herself to this new foreigner she had probably cast away the benefits and privileges of her former conversion. What should she do? She must, the proselyter said, expiate her sin, and being old, had better get to it quickly. To do this she must return to the husband by whom she was sold, he alone being her husband, that marriage being recorded in the proselyter's Heaven by his Lord. Having found him she would be doubly welcomed by the angels if before her death she achieved his conversion.

This pilgrimage did not appeal to the old lady. It was unreasonable, she felt, to exchange present security, although sinful, for unknown dangers of travel and virtue which through no fault of her own might remain beyond her reach. Should the husband be dead, as a widow without children, not knowing his relatives, she would have no place to go. Or, if the husband, now old, had another wife, perhaps many wives, she would find the situation awkward. Unwilling to dismiss completely all idea of a foreign Heaven, she delayed her decision, secretly conferring with her former pastor. To him she confessed her wickedness. Would his Lord also, like the proselyter's Lord, bar her from Heaven? She had been as good as a Chinese woman knew how to be. This missionary had lived long among her people, growing wise, considerate. He was sure, he told her, that his Lord made allowances for disparities between the marriage customs of China and those of the enlightened West. Not for an innocent mistake would she be punished. During the first gust of relief she not only returned to the church but forced a daughter-in-law to enroll in a Bible class.

She was pleased, was the wrinkled and almost bald old lady; but this pleasure

45

was not so vehement, so vigorous as is expected of one who narrowly misses eternal ostracism. Loudly she bewailed the fact that being too wicked for the proselyter's Heaven, which because of its exclusiveness was therefore undoubtedly superior in every way, she was compelled to resign herself to the prospects of a Presbyterian Paradise, more easily entered, therefore, second rate.

However, there is one compensation for a grandmother—the Proselyter's Lord has no free dispensary here below.

The Modern Young Man

H E IS a modern young man. He assures me of this in flawless English, sitting upon the deck, legs folded Buddha-fashion, as only an Oriental can. It is a fact patent to anybody. Instead of square-cornered Chinese garments, constricting the body nowhere, he wears a blue serge suit of Scotch weave, cut in Hong Kong by a British tailor. His feet, noticeably small, are conspicuous in American sport shoes, decorated with contrasting leather fancifully stitched. From a side pocket protrudes a soft Italian felt hat twisted into a cone. Altogether he is pleasant to look upon. His dark eyes, shadowed by thick fleshy lids, do not wince from the sunlight as mine do. Cowering beneath a hat brim I hug the miserable ribbon of noon-day shade lying along the cabin wall, while unaffected, he sits upon a blazing white scrubbed deck, with light raining from the sky, an inverted molten bowl, light incessantly caught and splintered upon the points of waves. His teeth shine, white and firm. His flesh, neither yellow nor white, is a smooth olive. To the body, supple and young, angularities are alien. Gestures trail gracefully from his fingertips. And about him there is a gaiety, a consistent gaiety, which at no time will get out of bounds, overflowing the reserve of his Oriental temperament.

46

Followers of upstart militarists—
always on borderline of banditry
R.B. Shantung
1919

By the event of last night, already gossiped about at breakfast in the Second Cabin, his gaiety may be intensified. I know nothing. I have heard that this charming youth came away from an all-night poker game in the First Cabin at dawn. Having won more than his passage to America he left behind him among others an enraged traveling salesman and a forlorn Australian bookie. Not one of your trumpery peddlers this salesman but a traveler in something big, locomotives, steel rails, tractors. It may be he directly above us, a heavy man with jowls, leaning upon the rail of the upper deck. The bookie, after seeing the Treaty Ports, is going to horse-races in Canada. At this hour upon any other day he and this Chinese youth have been playing mah jong for small stakes; but now he stands alone, blazer collar pulled up to his ears, staring at nothing. Usually so cheery, so needful of a sympathetic audience, there is something desolate in this isolation. But my companion glances neither at him nor towards the rail above.

This young man is fond of foreign dancing, but his performance as well as being curious is something of a scandal. The most intricate steps he has mastered. He is agile beyond any white man, but the white man's negroid rhythms do not enter into him. From first to last his stepping remains unrelated to the emphasis of the bass drummer. And at times his dancing is subtly impertinent. It was found so by two wan half-grown girls traveling from mission stations in a country which is not home to school in America, which is for them even a stranger land. When he asked them to dance again they refused, glancing at him with startled eyes. Privately the missionaries, of whom there are many among the passengers, scold; but he is guiltless, his mannerisms being common to those American dance-halls welcoming young Orientals.

To criticism by missionaries he would be indifferent. Already he tells me that he is an agnostic, adding to this the commonplace of Young China that missionaries are the tools of imperialism. He is modern in all things except in marriage. When he went away to an American college he had long been wed to an old-style girl of his mother's choice. Of a university degree he is no less

47

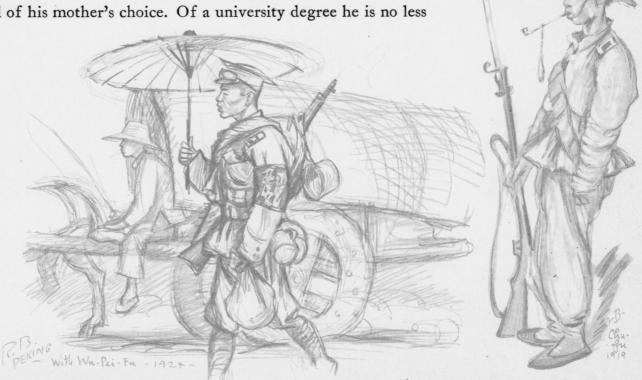

proud than of nine small children, mostly sons. But his business he deprecates. All up and down the land he goes, collecting cheap articles to be resold in America, matting trays, baskets, sleazy willow furniture, strings of beads, embroideries, scorning what he collects as beneath the taste of a cultured Chinese. Business is business, and if Americans demand from the Orient what they should, in his estimation, despise, it is not his affair.

More important than business, more important than the nine children, mostly sons, is his concern with New China. He is a Red, a member of the Kuo Ming Tang, an admirer of Russian communists, a former follower of the late Dr. Sun Yat Sen. Should he choose he could, he intimates, tell me a thing or two. He is occupied with thoughts from which I am excluded. Taking the pencil worn clipped to the edge of a breast pocket, he writes between the fine black lines of tar upon one narrow white scrubbed board of the deck figures necessary to some private computation which, however, he erases almost as soon as written.

New China will at the end of nine increasingly horrible years arise out of a China drenched with Chinese blood, he tells me. During the next six years revolution will follow revolution as fast as one military adventurer is able to crush another. But at the end of that period China will be conquered by the far North, made strong by Japanese aid. A stuffed doll upon a false throne, the Manchu ex-emperor will be restored, the mouthpiece of a Japanese dictatorship. China, unified by persecution, will, within three years, slaughter her traitors, cast off Japanese and Manchu. Out of this welter the New China will appear, a China of the people, not an aggressive nation, but strong enough to reclaim former possessions, Manchuria, Thibet, a province in northern India, Siam, Indo-China and the control of Korea!

What of the other nations? What of the Americans in China? I put the questions deferentially, awed by so much bloodshed. With one hand he makes a gesture of complete dismissal, he dusts all foreigners from the face of China. They must go, he says. However, the Chinese will not make any great effort to be rid of them. During increasing confusion international commerce will dwin-

48

Students
PEKING
— 24

The mellow note
of the Toy Makers'
gong rings distinct
to the child amid
the surge and
babble of the
streets

C LeRoy Baldridge
CHINA · 1925

dle. It may altogether vanish. Those few foreigners who have stubbornly held on will go gladly during a Japanese dictatorship.

I look at this lovely smiling lad sitting in the blazing sunlight. Why does he speak with the calm assurance of an oracle? This is easily explained. Had I examined the figures which he wrote upon the deck and then erased I would have read the specific dates given to him and to his radical friends in secret by the most honorable astrologer of Hong Kong! Can there be any room for doubt? asks this modern, this very modern young man.

 # I Am Told

DAY-LONG, night-long, tinkers hammer in their shops making ready stoves for those who can afford them. October will soon pass and, as in an ice-crystal, northern China will in winter be encased. During nights already chill, in a city vibrant with apprehension, this clamor is reassuring. Another revolution! In the north, Manchurian hordes gather for an assault upon Peking, I am told, drilled by tall Cossacks, by short Japanese, commanded by a hardy ex-bandit become a provincial official, having for aides a British hero of the Great War and an American buyer of modern supplies formerly attached to the diplomatic service. Of the hero it is said that having invented trench-mortars for his Chinese master, he has refused to make gas bombs, calling them uncivilized.

At Cook's the young man withers me. Of course the trains will continue to run so long as British capital is invested! Nevertheless, on the morrow there is one train only, an unscheduled train under international military guard, which carries the frightened tourists to Tientsin. The de luxe coaches of a famous express are already converted into barracks, seats torn out, stove-pipes thrust through the roofs.

49

Shanghai
'25

R. B.
Soochow
'25

Blind minstrels – in the past
neither pitiful nor beggarly
still belong to one of the
most ancient gilds.
ChRoy Baldwin E
PEKING T
25.

The blind
apprentice
sings of
Spring

Singers in the dark.
the blind minstrels
who perform while
others feast. –

C LeRoy Baldridge
PEKING – 1924

Rumors of the government's inevitable collapse exchanged across foreign dinner-tables in residences made almost inviolable by walls within walls and barred gates watched by gatemen, replace as topics the diverting perfidies of native servants. Business men bemoan losses from interrupted transportation, saying that in a month they make less than was earned before noon in the good old Imperial Days. And should there be danger, then, taking their jades and brocades, amber and pearls, table linens, porcelains, old brass and bronze, the foreigners will fly to the Legation Quarter, to the protection of foreign troops. To avert misunderstanding, they meanwhile hang above their gateway the flags of whatever treaty nations guarantee them safe-keeping, a warning to native troops that the sanctity with which foreign compounds have, since the Boxer uprising, been endowed, must be respected.

Forth go the government's dissimilar armies, the General Army led by a scholarly ex-bandit, the other by a man risen from the peasantry, famous for conversion to the Western faith, Peking's special guardian. Unpaid because of the government's bankruptcy, the untrained, undisciplined men of the former dribble out of the city gates. Ragged, without overcoats or blankets, carrying paper umbrellas and tin tea-pots, they escort wagons loaded with cumbrous chairs and tables for the use of officers, and military motors filled with sleek young women. Rations they will take by force from the farmers and with loot reward themselves. Much better off are their comrades wearing excellent uniforms, having overcoats, blankets, accompanied by munition wagons and camions, by modern commissaries. Marching they sing Protestant hymns and as talismans carry, I am told, New Testaments. Recently so many souls among them were saved that a foreign missionary administering baptisms was nearly prostrated. Moreover, they are paid. Concerning the source of this pay there is endless speculation.

Chinese-owned motors, seized by the military or hidden, disappear, also horses and carriages, donkeys and camels. To market comes a lad between the shafts of a heavy cart, drawing a load of cabbages, soldiers having taken his horse

52

en route. While the foreigners, their tough ponies exempt, play polo, the grocer across Hat-a-men Street loses his new Peking cart and fine white horse for which, copper by copper, he has been saving over a period of years. He shows a scrap of paper entitling him to horse and cart if when the battle ends he can find them. From caravans intercepted at the city gates the camels are taken, the brittle-legged beasts herded into open freight cars, gazing as is their wont at some point denied the vision of mankind.

Fewer coolies are seen, and not one man among the beggars. At Hsi-chi-men Gate, beyond which lie barracks, only small boys and horribly aged men offer rickshaws for hire. To protect rickshaw men in service from this conscription foreigners hang upon their vehicles their national flags, costing a pretty penny at the British shop. Ladies endlessly gyrating in the cycle of at-homes form a droll international pageant. So many coolies are taken against their will, without hope of remuneration, that the scholar-general needs must make a song about them which is something like this: They are our brothers, hired to help and carry out our commands as though real brothers. They work from morn till night, marching all the time. They are so tired and worn out, pity them. Among coolies are many as brave as we.

The armies go. The scholar-general, demanding funds, dallies. At last his train departs, attached to it a special car for foreign journalists. This car, cunningly side-tracked while they sleep, leaves them in an isolated village. They return. Cut off from the world Peking is enlivened from within by two journals, printing news in English, daily bestowing victories upon opposite sides. In a tantrum the government seals the presses of the one reporting defeats. Yet, it is well known that troops wounded by the modern guns of the Manchurians, abandoned by their scholar-general, have been rescued by foreign nurses and doctors, maggots in their wounds.

The government falls. His face drawn with fear, the cook brings the news with the breakfast coffee. The Manchurian has captured the city and the Central Government of the Chinese Republic, but in a most peculiar fashion.

53

These devoted indispensables
make the foreigner's residence
endurable on all occasions; and
their inexplicable perfidies
furnish endless anecdote at
tea, cocktail party and dinner —

CLeRoy Baldridge

PEKING
CHINA
25

In the name of his former enemy, betraying the scholar-general, betraying the government which he previously acknowledged, at night, unbeknownst to all except the tinkers, the convert returns and claims the capital! Among the missionaries, admirers say that despite criticism he acted to end further bloodshed. With this explanation the general placards the city. I am told that Chinese, mocking his religiosity, say that he uses Christianity to create solidarity among his troops, that he violates the Western code of honor and also a blood-brotherhood vow exchanged with his ally. More grave is the persistent gossip that an American engaged in semi-religious work, as financial and military counselor, is responsible for the whole affair. And again sums are named, enormous sums, received from the Japanese as bribes, shared by the general with the candidate for provisional presidency.

The Chinese are under martial law. Singing hymns, soldiers carry machine guns into Buddhist temples, into barracks, armed with cleaver-like executioners' axes patrol the gates. Upon the wall hangs the head of a looter. Night-long, day-long the tinkers hammer. In the Temple of the Jade Buddha the deposed president is reported to be kept, his brother and secretary thrown into a common jail. His brother, removed later to the foreign hospital, dies, some say of a chronic disease and others of abuse. The secretary, once a bath-steward, begins to disclose the uses to which public funds were put. But his testimony is never finished. Soldiers taking him from prison shoot him down in a public highway, a deed glorified as a political execution. Sequel to it there circulates a strange tale of a German and a Canadian who, locating the secretary's concubine, got from her ten thousand dollars of the stolen money, promising to save her lover. Upon his death she told the story to all who would listen and, while the German was abruptly dropped from a foreign firm, the Canadian, I am told, enjoys his prosperity.

Meanwhile, ex-officials scatter. Hospitals under foreign protection are besieged by Chinese gentlemen filled with pain, demanding treatment, paying well. As safe as in France they crowd into a Legation Quarter hotel, their

56

identity hidden behind names of English and American patriots. Sunday night when as is customary an old juggler in the hotel lounge draws bowls of goldfish from beneath his silk coat-tails, the lobby seethes with excited women, shrill children, sulky gentlemen. Ten people to a room, I hear, each paying the maximum price.

Foreigners prove extremely useful, storing the treasures of Chinese under the protection of their flags, escorting Chinese from place to place in defiance of martial law. A business man tells me of carrying two ex-officials disguised as rug dealers, in his car, beneath a British flag, through the Manchurian encampment to the super-safety of the Foreign Concessions in Tien-tsin. There, depositing his passengers upon a hotel doorstep, he collected one thousand Mexican dollars from each! Ribaldry is provoked by an important official's exit. Known to be an exquisite in matters of foreign dress, once the pet of Washington journalists and society, he escaped to a Treaty Port, I am told, in the hat and coat of an American woman, carried in a motor to the coast by her husband.

Such gentlemen leave behind beautiful homes, subject to confiscation by an incoming régime, in an effort to recover government funds. But foreigners, their holiness sanctifying their dwelling-places by occupation, protect these places. An obscure and genteel American, collector of carved hair-ornaments, tells me that he receives a monthly salary, his living, a motor, in return for occupying a palace and raising an American flag above the door. The business man, in addition to transporting Chinese, has five such houses, he tells me, a British flag above each, additionally secured by leases and mortgages of doubtful value. Innocently, two travellers marooned in the capital accept, rent-free, the elegant quarters of a Chinese gentleman, their tenancy made regular by a lease, the only purpose of occupancy protection from looting by soldiers; he being compelled to go for the sake of misplaced political loyalties!

The cook, eyes distended, announces that in violation of the Republic's agreement the convert-general has evicted the young Manchu ex-emperor and his two wives from the rotting grandeur of the Forbidden City which by decree

imprisoned them. To the Americans comes the news of a president's re-election! But what of that? Poor little emperor, poor, dull-witted lad, poor Mr. Pu Yi. The convert-general's defenders wag their heads over a frustrated royalist plot. The skeptical ask, what became of the royal treasures? And the general, making way for the Provisional Government, retires to a Buddhist Temple in the Western Hills, sending daily messages of sweetness to his former ally, discredited, bankrupt, retreating southward.

Without elections the new government proceeds, its national conference attended by proxies, the fearsome old radical from the South who threatened it dying from a mortal illness, leaving successors in Russian blouses. The journal's presses, released again, reveal the source of the paper's subsidy—Manchuria. Shaken is a foreign group by the sudden departure of an American, his name too often linked with that of the convert-general.

April. Motors, horses and carriages, donkeys and camels are upon the streets. At Hsi-chi-men Gate husky coolies offer rickshaws for hire. From house to house go the tinkers taking down stove-pipes, covering stove-holes with discs of tin. After a fashion transportation is restored. And the two who live in the elegant quarters of the private citizen cancel their lease, eager to be off. Their landlord, hiding in Japan, they have learned, is an ex-official, charged with monstrous rapacity; his Chinese pavilions, monuments to graft; the lease mere paper; the virtue of their occupancy as Americans, dubious. Delight in pearl-inlaid teakwood, in walls of carved wood and blue silk, becomes guilty. In order to avoid complicity in a compatriot's unsuccessful attempt to seize the house for some mysterious agent, upon no authority except his foreign citizenship, they leave precipitously. Paved courtyards and willow tree, stone carvings, the lotus pool, the ancestral shrine with cloisonné brazier and candlesticks, for these, as they go, the police and the Manchurians contend, the former attempting confiscation in the name of the government, the latter demanding restitution for an old theft in the name of their master.

Of this I need not be told. For of the departing two, I am one.

58

The ancient city of slow-moving
evil-smelling canals which pass
beneath arched bridges of exquisite
grace —

RAIN, slanting rain, across the windows, beating upon the roof, dripping through the roof to the floor of the Third Class railroad coach. With April rain the air outside is wet, sweet. Within, stale, sour, rank with the odor of damp cotton garments, not over-clean, with odors of ducks and chickens stowed beneath the seats in wooden boxes, in baskets, in sacks. Baby chicks chirp insistently like crickets. Up one side and down the other, wooden benches. Back to back down the car's center, two more wooden benches. Two double rows of cotton laps, not always the same laps, not always continuous. Listless, half-asleep, wholly asleep are the passengers, all of them men. Friends who enter together talk together. Strangers do not speak. Whenever possible full length, their hands in their sleeves, passengers stretch out upon the benches unchallenged by those who, finding no seats, must stand huddled together at either end of the car. No one reads. Many have sore eyes. Almost everybody has a cold. There is constant coughing and no handkerchiefs. There are no cuspidors as in the First Class.

Slowly, slowly, towards Shanghai the train crawls, stops, waits. After a time freight cars pass filled with tatterdemalion soldiers, among them always a few dispirited blonde Russians, the mercenaries of provincial militarists, moving towards another local revolution. No interest seems awakened by the passing of these troops or by the young, bullet-headed ruffian, a soldier, who, swaggering through the car without reason, forces aside the laps, treading upon feet in cotton shoes, knocking against the passengers with his thermos flask and gun butt. No protest, no glance rewards this performance.

From a charcoal stove in a corner of the verminous lavatory the tea-boy brings hot water for tea, and chipped enamel basins of food. Constantly he distributes, collects and refills for redistribution the white crockery tea-pots, wiping out the small bowls which serve as cups with a scrawny rag, sodden and grimy. It has

59

other uses. With it he alternately mops the sweat from his face and neck, mops a space upon the bench which serves as a cupboard. Otherwise it is twisted into the belt of his trousers, beneath his coat. Many of those who buy tea for a few coppers do not use the bowls, drinking in a droll fashion from the spouts, friends sharing spouts, between drinks the pots being set upon the floor, underfoot, hidden by the skirts of long cotton coats. Forcing aside the laps the tea-boy offers for sale eggs which have been boiled hard in a liquid resembling strong tea which has been spiced, and bundles of cakes soaked in the same liquid. In the other wash-basin are bulbs which have been boiled, having an earthy odor and called "water chestnuts." Enormous quantities of cakes are eaten, also eggs, the shells littering the floor. Ripped off with the teeth the brown covering of the bulbs is spat forth.

Rain upon the windows, rain upon the roof, increasing slime beneath my feet. Passengers cough, spit, converse, sleep, drink tea, eat eggs and bulbs. Treading upon feet, the glowering soldier boy crushes the indifferent passengers.

The train crawls, waits, and, after the passing of troops, crawls again.

Shanghai! It was to have been such a short trip, less than seven daylight hours and in the Third Class, so cheap. It is cheap.

Night presses upon the windows. The train crawls, waits, crawls. The flat country, the troops, are no longer to be seen for darkness. The passengers sleep, stiffly upright and unswaying, bodies accustomed to wooden planks for beds lying rigid but comfortable upon the benches. Seven hours pass, eight hours, thirteen hours. Eighteen!

Shanghai!

It is long after midnight. Wind sweeps through the railroad station, empty except for furtive, disreputable foreign men seeking shelter, creatures of the night. Quickly the passengers disappear, carried away in wobbling rickshaws by unkempt coolies, in private motor cars. No taxicabs. One fine motor waits, but no one comes. The driver, a Chinese as dapper as any returned student, for one Mexican dollar offers to go to the address named. He does not, however, con-

60

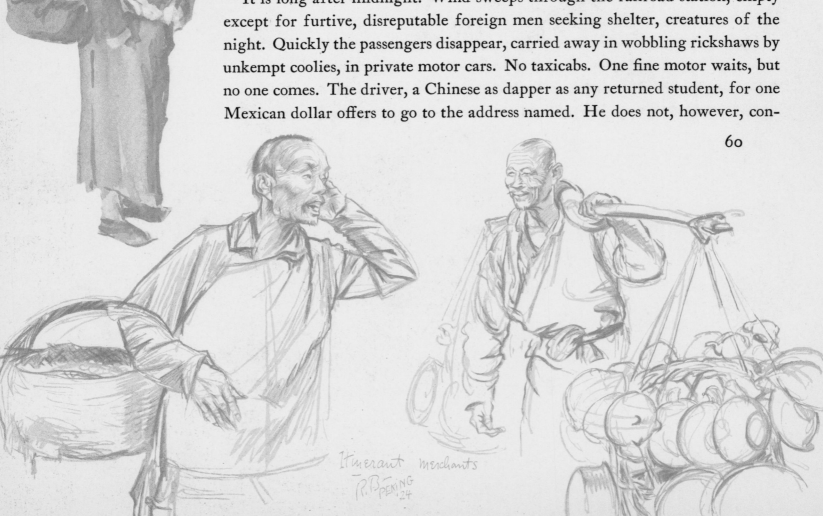

Itinerant merchants
R. B. PEKING '24

All the commodities of life
are hawked from door-way to
doorway down the crooked
streets.

C LeRoy Baldridge.
- PEKING '24

Shrewd and canny
begging priests who
live by their wits —

In a temple obscured
by foreign ships,
the chants

Ming Tombs
'24

Shanghai 1919

Spring, and the Taoist
pilgrim priest rambled
over the summit of
the sacred Mountain
singing for joy.

A century old,
blind, forgotten
by life in a half-
ruined temple

Already attached
to half dead
religious orders.

T'ai Cheh Ssŭ '24   Harvest moon festival

C. LeRoy Baldridge.
Tai-Shan '25

6,600 Steps up through the South Gate
of Heaven and back again in a day trudge
provincial pilgrims, old men, women with
bound feet, rich riding in chairs carrying
fire crackers to the temples and money
for beggars infesting the cliffs —

C. LeRoy Baldridge
Tai-shan – 25.

descend to the luggage; the two knobby knapsacks; a large suitcase; a small suitcase; a lovely Chinese basket from a temple fair in Peking, said to be of those brought to the city in ancient times filled with food and writing materials by candidates for the classical examinations; and a hamper.

The cool, wet air lays refreshing hands upon forehead, eyelids, cheeks. The upholstered cushions are luxurious. In less than a half-hour there will be the security of a friend's house, the clean white bed, the hot bath and something to eat. I am hungry. As a boat upon the waters of black canals the motor skims over the surface of wet asphalt streets, gleaming beneath street lamps. Shuttered European shops, modern business houses rise dimly upon the banks. Rows of modern houses, side walls joined, tall houses in gardens. The car stops.

It stands before a large white building distended with light. Against the heavy air a jazz band bleats and brays through an open window. This is not the address agreed upon. But the driver who was so fluent has ceased altogether to speak or understand English. An interpreter must be got before he will proceed.

But no help is to be had from the Irish-American resort keeper, from the Russian bartender, from the Sikh "bouncer," black-skinned, bearded, turbaned. Diverted by two bedraggled human beings standing in St. ———'s roadhouse asking for St. ———'s mission school, the Russian ladies, the French ladies, the American ladies take their pretty slippered feet from the tables, gather 'round, some of them a trifle unsteadily upon pretty silken legs. The music bleats again. They ride away out over the dance floor upon the chests of American business men, Britishers, Europeans. Only the Chinese headwaiter remembers having seen the school upon the Settlement's edge, one of the oldest, one of the largest, one of the most popular mission schools in China. It is he who confers with the driver. Some day this episode will, I am sure, be funny.

The rain, no longer misty, is heavy, sullen, chill. Whirling through the open car it drenches coats, hats, luggage. The motor skims no longer over dark asphalt but rides upon good dirt roads between houses and gardens, houses and gardens, over uneven dirt roads between small huts and into open country where for long

64

stretches there are no huts at all. This is China! Not here in the open country, but in a settled district upon the Foreign Settlement's edge, the mission school lies. This wild ride must end. With great effort the name of a hotel is recalled, a hotel patronized once by journalists and clerks, suited to Third Class passengers, being modest, having the atmosphere of a pension de famille. The driver, now surly, turns the car about.

Dirt roads and little huts. Dirt streets and foreign houses within gardens. The resort distended with light. Wet asphalt streets like black canals. Shuttered shops and tall buildings. The hotel.

Slowly and with a fearful silence in what appears to be a solid wall a small square opening is revealed by the drawing aside of a panel. Silhouetted against a light there appears the custodian of the establishment's peace, a Sikh, swarthy, bearded and in a scarlet turban. Fixed with amazement I, who am closest to him, do not move within the car. Hearing nothing, perceiving nothing irregular, he withdraws his head. The square is closed. In the darkness the wall appears once more to be solid. Pension de famille, indeed!

It is not the hotel which it once was, having fallen into the hands of new owners. For a staggering price quoted by the Chinese night-clerk a bedroom may be had for the few remaining hours of night and a few hours following sunrise. Openly the two porters scorn the amazing hand-luggage.

Now the driver must be attended to. He names a price, also staggering, answering the protest with insolence. He is voluble. The jist of what he says is that there may be in the city a school under the patronage of another saint than the one for whom the resort is named. However, he does not believe that travelling American couples found upon the streets after midnight seek mission schools. It has been his experience that they desire good singsong houses. Therefore this night he went speedily to the best foreign singsong house; but it did not suit. Had he not been ordered to turn back he would soon have got to another far outside the Settlement, one managed by an American for Americans. This he stated in English, somewhat confused, but decisive and exceedingly

65

Police—
Foreign Settlement
1919—

vulgar. After this tirade one silver dollar was thrust into his hand, the hotel doors finally closed upon his horrid squealing and his Western profanity.

Shanghai!

In the dining-room a band bleats and brays American jazz. French ladies, Russian ladies, and Americans, their pretty silken legs upon the tables, blow smoke into the eyes of American business men, British, Europeans, or ride this way and that way across the polished floor leaning upon the bosoms of dinner shirts .

Through Broken Reed and Bamboo

A CLUTTERED labyrinth is this department store. From electric bulbs set at every angle shrill light streams. It echoes and reechoes from polished brass, glass planes, from countless mirrors. Walking back and forth through every aisle, climbing up and down the staircases, riding up and riding down again in the elevators, are family parties of nouveau riche. By the hands silken papas lead putty-faced male children who are eternally munching. Trailing after come bejewelled female children and the women whose fashionable coats with wide sleeves ending above the wrists, flaring abruptly over the hips, are reminiscent of Victorian "dressing sacques." The looking, looking, pointing, ejaculating of the sightseers transforms the shop into a museum.

Everywhere are displayed tawdry and perishable imitations of European products, also Oriental objects degraded by quantity production and by the substitution of machinery for craftsmen. And yet, beauty, doomed amid jig-saw carvings, rugs with designs stencilled instead of woven, porcelain Goddesses of Mercy baked in molds like so many muffins and not modelled by individual potters, still survives with incredible vitality in occasional forms and decorations.

66

R.B.
'25

Just outside the
Foreign Settlement — China
R.B. Shanghai
'25

The Peking walls though grass grown and neglected,
are not yet robbed 'by time of dignity and majesty!

CLeRoy Baldridge - PEKING -25

Gazing, equally fascinated by all things, the silken papas and their families pass through every department, mounting finally to a restaurant or to the roof with its soda fountain, and a small auditorium where native story-tellers alternate with actors whose buffoonery is faintly European, and where from a promenade among potted plants they may have an excellent view of the foreign race course.

I, too, mount upwards, following a young Chinese radical who flings across his shoulder in not too tolerable English his newly acquired opinions about minimum wages, child labor, free speech. Eventually, we also arrive at one of the restaurants and are seated in a small private dining-room adjoining the banquet hall, a not particularly favorable place in which to spend a last evening in China. Its privacy is formed by four low walls, painted white, but dusty and finger-marked. Upon the varnished sideboard the glassware is dull. Linoleum of a dark green and brown patterns covers the floor. Hung askew upon the table is a cloth, rough with cotton lint and in need of bleaching. Also there are three large brass cuspidors without which Chinese elegance is neither complete nor comfortable. From the adjoining banquet hall the room is filled with a deafening cacophony, for business men and their wives are celebrating the wedding of a merchant's daughter to a merchant's son. This the radical tells me with a fine scorn, because in his grandfather's day even the peasant farmer was among the socially elect, while the merchant remained considerably beyond the pale. There is falsetto singing of hired performers, crashing of brass cymbals and beating of drums, the whine of one-stringed violins, laughter, a fury of conversation, and the incessant jangling of forks and knives against crockery. But out of this bedlam the bank clerk whom I await will eventually emerge.

I ought to be impatient for the moment of his arrival, but I am not. To a degree little divined by his friend, the young radical, my curiosity has subsided since first I heard of him in another city. Then he was pictured to me as an obscure young man whose passionate devotion to musical research had by its intensity fused together the interests of several hundred youths for more than six years, flowering into the recognizable beginnings of a musical renascence.

67

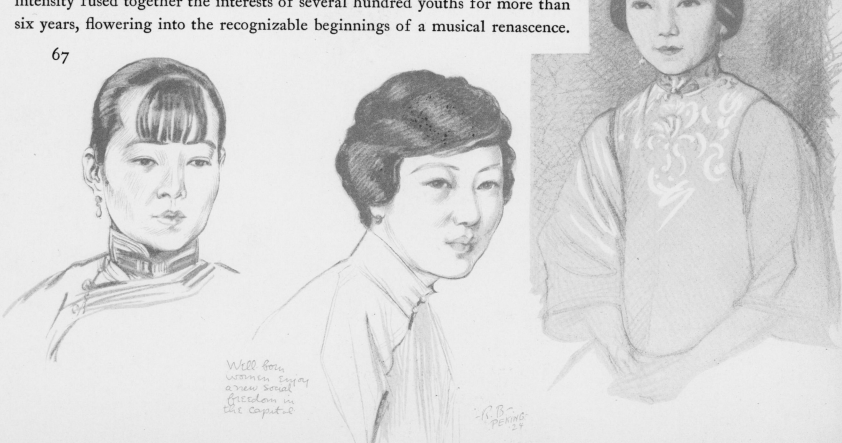

Well born
women enjoy
a new social
freedom in
the capital

B
PEKING
24

There was so much charm about the tale that it seemed a legend; and upon reaching Shanghai I asked for the truth. I was told that the young man was not a legendary figure but a very real bank clerk whom I would find perched upon a long-legged stool, his eyes glued to a ledger page, his job the counting of money belonging to the silken papas. Thereupon curiosity ebbed from me. Already I have met clumsy-minded gentlemen of this new age, men with money-bags in their hands as well as the petards which once belonged solely to the scholars, declaring themselves to be artists or the patrons of art. Truly, anticipation stirs me very little; but the food—

Gluttony is a sweet vice. No longer do I look with scornful eyes upon those pot-bellied fellows, overflowing with fat like squatting Buddhas, their lips grown heavy and pendulous with rich living and seeming always a little moist from the last delectable sauce. This chicken with noodles, made savory by garlic and dark strips of some fungus, is an emotional experience. The low white bowl from which I pluck it with metal chopsticks is enchanting. By squinting I can resolve the splashes of black and color upon the sloping sides into butterflies and peonies. Preoccupied with these delights I do not at once discover a young man standing beside me, his fingertips resting upon the table. He is small and wears dark foreign clothes. Beneath one arm is crushed a foreign hat, and gold chains flop upon his waistcoat. The bank clerk has come.

His hands are unbelievably delicate, hands not destined for the mauling of gold. And his eyes are focussed upon dream-beclouded horizons beyond the boundaries of any ledger page. Hurriedly I fumble in my mind for some phrase which, if quickly translated by the radical, will arrest him. He is already poised for flight. I state dogmatically that Chinese music is baffling, shallow, and only rarely provocative. Scarcely a pretty speech, but effective. The shy bank clerk becomes vivid. Words, Chinese monosyllables with every shade of inflection, pour from him. His hands rise and fall. He pushes away from his forehead the black hair, curiously finer than is usual and not pomaded as is fashionable with young men of the business world.

68

Apprentices
Great Wall
RB
1925

Wandering
troupe of
child
actors

To the
accompaniment
of topical
song's the
monkey
dances

Story teller
at Temple fair
1919

Modelling familiar stage
figures out of colored dough

C. LeRoy Baldridge
— PEKING CHINA/ 25

Market at Temple Entrance
Tai-yüan-fu

By day he is a bank clerk; by night a mathematician, an amateur scientist, experimenting with sound waves, leader of a musical movement, author of twelve books upon the history of Chinese music. The counting house for him by day, at all other times the high adventure of recovering China's past. The music, which I, like any other traveller, have heard, is that of the theater, the tea-house, the blind minstrels. This, in his opinion, has been decadent, corrupt, more Tartar and barbarian than Chinese for two thousand years. Its dissonances are without purpose, occurring only because centuries ago, during revolutions and invasions, musicians lost the standard pitch which once guided them all in tuning their instruments. Buried in these dissonances he occasionally discovers fragments of pure melody, their origin unknown, inherited by minstrels from their masters century after century. These he preserves to support his belief that once Chinese music was composed according to major scales identical with those of the West. Recently a manuscript, obviously old, found in the hands of a junk dealer, after resisting deciphering for many months, became intelligible when played in minor keys, proof for him that, as major scales once existed, so also there were minor scales.

Upon what, I ask, feeds this young man's intensity? The dark eyes return from their far horizons to me. His belief! When the music of the East is recovered, then will the East understand its own soul, now filled with confusion. Then, also, will the West understand the East and peaceful international adjustments become possible. Mathematics are universal; music must also be. For in East and West sound waves are identical and strike in an identical manner upon the ears of Chinese or Europeans, stimulating, he is certain, dreams less dissimilar than is believed.

A student has told him that already modern art in Europe is akin to the best painting of China. There will soon be sympathetic approaches in other arts. Is there not already a prophecy of this in modern French music? But when the music of China is recaptured, the West must not seize upon it, recast it for foreign instruments. With Chinese poetry it shares singleness of thought, sim-

71

True to Confucian tradition the classical scholar plays a lute.

R.B.
PEKING 24

plicity of presentation. Solo in quality it must remain. The young bank clerk looks at me with dark, troubled eyes and speaks to me with the aid of his friend; but he is looking through me at alien shores and, in this grubby room of a department store, pleads with alien people gathered upon them.

We are all three of us inexpressibly fatigued. One of us knows no English; one of us knows no Chinese; and one of us speaks English only tolerably. There have been delays, misunderstandings, repetitions. It is as if for hours we had been groping, seeking to communicate through fog as tangible as blanket wool, revealed to each other now and then for a brief moment.

The night is half done. Long ago the guests of the merchant went away. The silken papas, mouthing toothpicks, followed by their families, flow torpidly towards the exits. In their midst we debouch into the business street of the Foreign Settlement. We are to part. The bank clerk hesitates. I am told that he wishes to speak again.

The flute, he says, was man's first instrument. The first flute in Europe was a broken hollow reed through which the wind sang, until man, enchanted, took the reed for his own instrument. Likewise, in China, the wind sang to man through a broken bamboo. Through hollow reed or bamboo the wind's song is the same song. It is not absurd for him to believe that notes of the bamboo would be pleasing to the Western ear. If the foreign woman could hear the flute played properly, perhaps if she would learn to play it herself—

His dark hair flying, the bank clerk, small and slight, is engulfed by the monstrous shadows of modern office buildings.

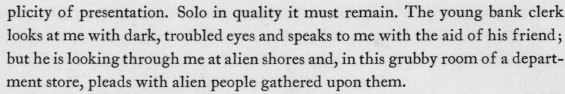

Today I sail away. The great white ship reaches for its passengers with long-armed gangplanks and cranes, while all about its bulk, like water insects, dart small native boats. I turn to the West carrying three flutes which came this morning from the bank clerk, and which he carved himself from bamboo. Blowing upon the smallest I evoke a single note.

Out of all proportion to my effort, it is thin and faint.

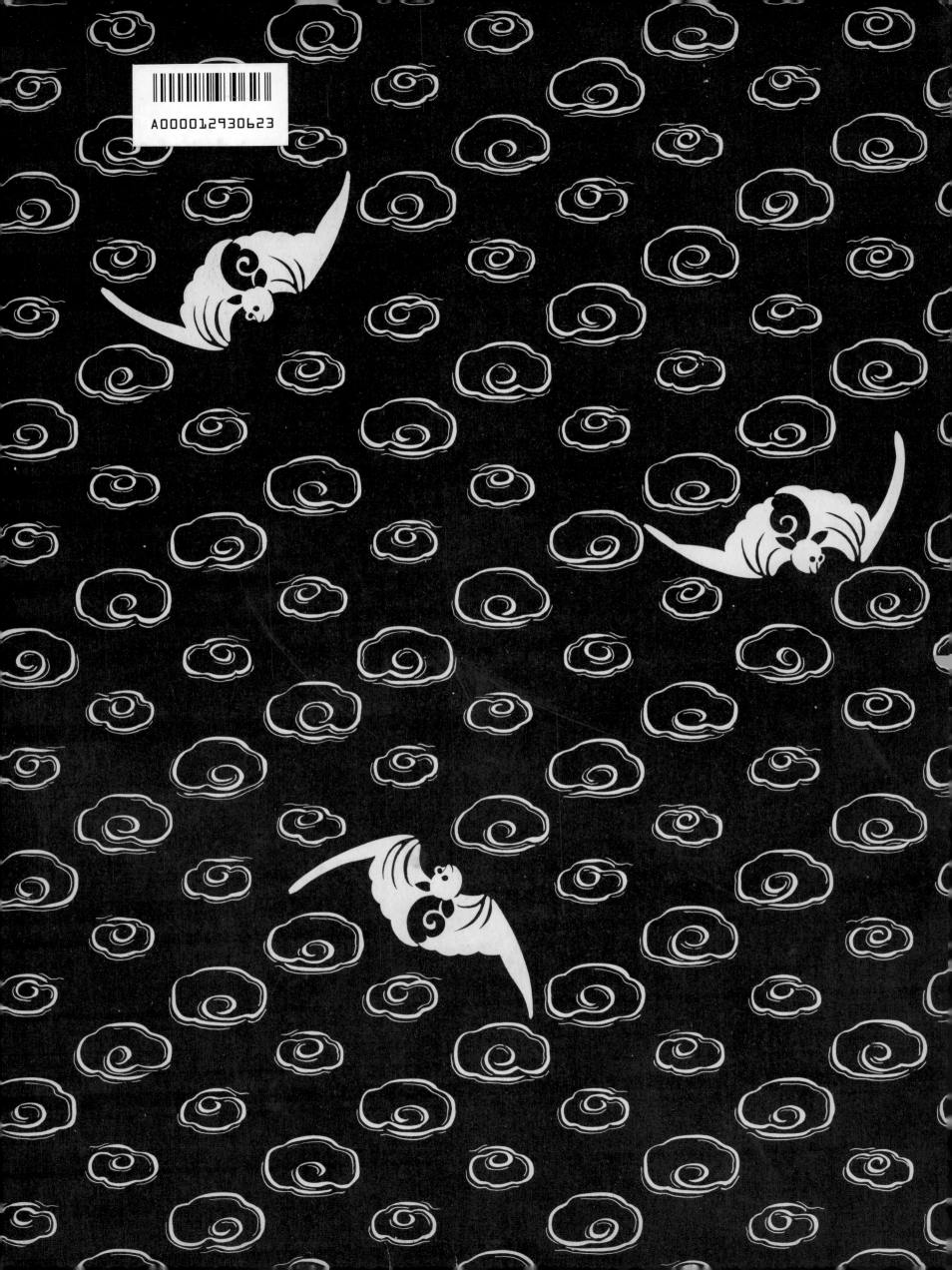